JTELY

HING

A

GH!

ANYTHING FOR A LAUGH

A Collection of Jokes and
Anecdotes That You, Too, Can
Tell — and Probably Have

EDITED BY
BENNETT CERF

Cartoons By O'CONNOR BARRETT

BANTAM BOOKS New York

Every year, at least ten new collections of jokes and anecdotes are offered to the public. During the past decade, the pace has been accelerated. People were hungry for anything that would make them laugh and allow them to forget momentarily the manifold troubles of the world in which they lived. The questions anybody might reasonably ask are: one, why should some of these collections prove so much more popular than others; and, two, where on earth do all the jokes that fill them come from?

I have been regaling my frequently unamused friends with stories and quips ever since I edited Columbia's humorous monthly, *The Jester*, some twenty-seven years ago, but never realized the commercial potentialities of this very questionable knack until my *Pocket Book of War Humor*, hurriedly whipped up to fill an obvious demand, amazed the publishers and myself by selling something like a million and a half copies. On top of that, *Try and Stop Me*, a collection of trivia originally designed to be a companion to the war humor book (at the same price) proved again that people wanted amusing stories, be they brand new or as old as the hills.

Suddenly I found myself an "authority" on this sort of thing. Total strangers began sending me their favorite stories and old collections they had treasured on their shelves. One good soul sent me a wooden packing case full of yellowing joke books that dated back a hundred years and more. Friends buttonholed me on the street and began, "Here's one I bet you haven't heard yet." (I discovered they liked me better when I agreed I had not.) *Life* magazine bestowed upon me the dubious title of "The Nation's Number One Peddler of Jokes."

I have discovered that this sudden acceptance as an authority on old jokes, or "Joe Miller of 1946," does not sit easily on my shoulders. I am a book publisher by choice; I would rather be remembered as the publisher of Eugene O'Neill, Sinclair Lewis, William Faulkner, and James Joyce's *Ulysses* than a facile raconteur or anthologist of other people's bons mots. *Anything for a Laugh* and a sequel to *Try and Stop Me* in a year or so (already contracted for and tentatively titled *Shake Well Before Using*) will be the last books of this sort that will bear my name for a long time to come.

There is more to the compilation of a good joke book than mere application of scissors and paste. Successes are the result of judicious selection, timing, balance, and variety. Failures are the ones that are thrown together in haphazard fashion by careless editors who do not even bother to reword their material or bring it up to date. In some of the poorer anthologies I have examined in the past few years, I can show you the same jokes, word for word, repeated over and over again. The better collections, the ones that have sold, are at least reconditioned and freshened. They are presented with some sense of pace and quality. The wisecracks and rapid-fire gags are balanced always by more subtle and gentle types of humor. No one group or class is singled out for ridicule. A careful course is steered between bad taste on the one hand and stiff-backed Puritanism on the other. I have tried to bear these things in mind in the following pages.

Now for the question of where the jokes come from. These are my principal sources:

1. Stories told to me by friends or sent to me by benevolent contributors.

2. Stories brought to mind by the new ones I hear. All of you undoubtedly will recall instances where one

story suddenly reminded you of a half-dozen others.

3. Stories I have used during the past year in my "Trade Winds" column in the *Saturday Review of Literature* and my "Back of the Book" column in *Omnibook*. (An editor once told Charles Poore, "If you know a good story, publish it from time to time.")

4. Radio jokes. Dozens of high-powered writers are beating their brains out every week to provide famous comics with reasonably fresh material. I do not have time to listen to more than one or two of these programs a week, but the big networks very kindly send out press sheets containing the best of the new quips, in the sound belief that the oftener they are reprinted, the more publicity will redound to the personalities involved. You will find a lot of these stories herein, properly credited.

5. Old joke books and files. Several professionals have files of thousands and thousands of funny stories; a few have allowed me to thumb through them. For the most part this is a dreary and unrewarding procedure, but I have found an occasional story that could be modernized and that made me laugh.

6. Syndicated columns. There are more columnists in New York today than there are night clubs on Fifty-second Street. There is small likelihood that a fresh story will escape the eagle eyes of all of them. Sometimes two or more will pounce on a choice bit at the same time. When Maurice Evans opened his revival of *Hamlet*, for instance, a jolly and popular restaurateur named Toots Shor observed that he was the most fortunate member of the opening night audience: he was the only one who didn't know how the play was going to end! This sally was dutifully reported in no fewer than three columns the following day—two of them in the same newspaper.

When I compiled *Try and Stop Me* I innocently

assumed that, as I had contributed stories for years to both Walter Winchell and Leonard Lyons, they would have no objection to my using with due credit some of theirs. This proved, however, to be a gross miscalculation on my part. It developed that when *they* used other people's stories it was called "originating"; when *I* used them it was called "anecdote stealing." I discovered also that these gentlemen were very good at claiming credit for stories they heard or read in exactly the same places that I did. Accordingly, I have been particularly careful in these pages not to take one story from either the Winchell or Lyons columns, though some of them undoubtedly have appeared there—or will later. There are stories here dug up by Louis Sobol, Earl Wilson, Sid Skolsky, and Irving Hoffman—courtesies which I hope to repay in kind.

A late Archbishop of Canterbury declared once, "Every time a man smiles, and much more so when he laughs, something is added to this fragment of life." It is in that spirit that I offer you these stories—edited, rewritten, dry-cleaned, arranged, and equipped with this year's license plates—by a prattle-scarred veteran who is about ready to try and stop himself.

BENNETT CERF

New York
September, 1946

IN THE days when Britain stood alone against the might of Nazi Germany, Winston Churchill was the symbol and the mouthpiece of her resolution. His star has dimmed since then—but the magic of his oratory has not. You may no longer like what he is saying, but you have to admire the way he says it!

On his recent visit to America, Churchill told of an historic night at the White House. He had retired to his room after a long conference with President Roosevelt and Harry Hopkins and was posturing before the mirror, completely naked, rehearsing a speech for the morrow, when there came an imperative knock on his door. The President had thought of a new angle, and couldn't even wait until morning to discuss it.

Churchill listened respectfully, then enthusiastically. "I will back you in this step all the way," he declared to FDR and Hopkins (who had come with him). "And I would like to add that this is probably the first time a Prime Minister of Britain ever received the head of a great foreign power in the absolute nude."

Mr. Churchill would neither confirm nor deny the story of an audience given by the King and himself to an American banker at a time when the outlook was blackest for England. "London is being raided nightly," the King is supposed to have said. "Rommel may capture Suez. India is in ferment. Japan menaces Australia. What to do, what to do?"

The American considered gravely and then suggested, "Your Majesty, if I were you, I'd put Canada in the Queen's name!"

A soldier disembarked in San Francisco after two long years in the Far East, and was greeted with appropriate ecstasy by his beautiful young wife. Alone at last in their room at the Mark Hopkins Hotel, they were disturbed by a sudden clamor in the corridor, and a cry of "Let me in!"

The soldier jumped four feet and exclaimed, "I'll bet it's your husband." The beautiful young wife answered angrily, "Don't be silly. He's thousands of miles away somewhere in the Pacific!"

Of all the animals in the Bronx Park Zoo, Mrs. Bibbledoffer liked the gnus best. What it was about them, she could not explain, but she found herself unable to tear herself away from their enclosure.

When a keeper sauntered by, Mrs. Bibbledoffer

stopped him. "What enchanting animals gnus are," she enthused. "Are they vicious? Do they bite?"

"Lady," said the keeper tersely, "the motto of this zoo is 'No Gnus Is Good Gnus.'"

A man in Glencoe bought a million 1942 calendars for a penny apiece. "What on earth are you going to do with them?" he was asked. "It's rather a long chance, I admit," he said, "but, oh boy, if 1942 ever comes back, I'll make a fortune."

For years Old Man Commins revelled in the reputation of being the most unfortunate patient of St. Mary's Hospital. He had rheumatism and St. Vitus' Dance at the same time, and people came from miles to watch and pity him. But wasn't Old Man Commins' nose put out of joint when they brought Mr. Miller in on a stretcher! Mr. Miller, it seems, got a case of severe seasickness and lockjaw at the same time.

An American soldier, standing outside Notre Dame Cathedral in Paris, saw a magnificent wedding procession enter. "Who's the bridegroom?" he asked a Frenchman standing next to him. "*Je ne sais pas*," was the reply. A few minutes later, the soldier inspected the interior of the cathedral himself, and saw a coffin being carried down the aisle. "Whose funeral?" he demanded of an attendant. "*Je ne sais pas*," said the attendant. "Holy mackerel," exclaimed the soldier. "He certainly didn't last long."

A big Eastern state recently elected a governor who was a model of statesmanship and integrity, but unfortunately had the kind of face that an unkind friend described as "an accident on its way to happen." The Governor himself quoted Jimmy Durante's witticism, "I'm not handsome, but I'm unique."

One evening the Governor was motoring alone in a very sparsely settled corner of the state when a torrential downpour made the roads impassable. He sought shelter at the nearest farmhouse, where the master, obviously failing to recognize his visitor, said in a friendly enough tone, "We ain't equipped to handle visitors, but in weather like this we wouldn't turn out nobody. If you don't mind sleeping with my young son, you're welcome to stay the night."

The boy took the grateful Governor up to his room and turned on the lamp. Three photographs decorated the wall. On the left was a picture of Washington, on the right a picture of Lincoln, and squarely in the middle, a large picture of the Governor himself!

"Well, son," said the Governor, "who is that fine looking gentleman in the corner?" "That," was the reply, "is George Washington, the father of our country." "And the one in the other corner?" "That's Abraham Lincoln, who freed the slaves." "And the distinguished man in the center?" The boy frowned, and said, "Gee, Mister, I haven't the least idea. Ma hung it there to show me what I'll look like when I grow up if I keep on playing hookey all the time!"

The shortest, and one of the most effective editorials on the unveiling of the atomic bomb consisted of exactly two sentences: "The atomic bomb is here to stay. But are we?"

The workers at Oak Ridge, Tennessee, where the bomb was perfected, maintained perfect secrecy to the very end. Their favorite explanation for the presence of the huge, closely guarded installations was "This is where we make the fronts of horses. Then we ship them to the Pentagon Building for final assembly."

News of the bomb reminded one wit of the farmer whose son came home from Massachusetts Tech and said his class was trying to find a universal solvent. "What's that?" asked the farmer. "It's a liquid that will dissolve everything," explained the son. "Great idea," nodded the farmer. "But when you find it, *what you gonna keep it in?*"

The man in the barber chair signalled with his finger. "Got another razor?" he whispered. "Why?" asked Vincent, the barber. "I'd like to defend myself," said the customer.

Another group invented an atom bomb so powerful that it could destroy the world. They couldn't resist trying it just once. When the smoke had cleared away, the only two things left alive on the face of the earth were two monkeys somewhere in Tibet. The male monkey leered at his companion, and said, "Well, shall we start the whole thing all over again?"

The senatorial investigation of the atom bomb was so innocuous, the questions so carefully phrased, that it reminded Drew Pearson of the gate-tender's testimony after the Chicago Express demolished an automobile at the crossing he guarded. He swore to the court that he had waved his lantern vigorously; the jury believed him and awarded the verdict to the railroad. Later his attorney said, "See, Tom, you weren't nervous on the stand after all, were you?" "Only once," confessed the gate-tender. "If that fellow had asked me if the lantern was lit, we wouldn't have had a chance."

Colonel Sartoris Beauregard Munchausen, of the Louisville branch of the celebrated family, declared that his mare Honeysuckle was the greatest racehorse of all time. Proof? The Colonel, with a far-away look in his eyes, would soak his feet in a pail of mint juleps, and reminisce, "I remember, suh, a race of sixteen thorough- breds in which my mare Honeysuckle participated. The stake was three hundred thousand dollars. Gentlemen who owned the best horse-flesh in all the South were present, not to mention a few Yankees. Well, suh, Honeysuckle was leading the field, which was no sur- prise to me, when on the backstretch I noticed her hesitate. And then and there she had herself a foal. I had bred her the year before, but didn't know she was foaling."

At this point, someone in the audience would sympa- thize, and say "Tough way to lose a race."

"Who said anything about losing?" the good Colo- nel would conclude. "Honeysuckle never lost. She had her foal. Then she won the race by five lengths."

"And," he added, "the foal came in second."

A G.I. with the occupation troops in Germany re- ceived a cable from his girl that deserves a medal for the prize "short short story" of the year. It read, "Couldn't wait for you so have married your father. Love, Mother."

Another soldier who had been abroad for three years, and heard that he was being shipped home, wired his girl, "Better take some tetanus shots, honey. I've gotten rusty."

Pundits tell us that Allah refrained from deducting from the allotted time of man those hours spent in fishing. If Allah was in his right mind, however, he'd deduct thirty years from the perpetrator of the follow- ing mess of piscatorial puns:

The prettiest she-fish in the whole aquarium was Bess Porgy. Young John Haddock's gills fluttered with suppressed poisson every time she, and her chubby friend, Mazie Angelfish, slithered down the pike. To kipper in comfort was his consuming obsession.

Trouble loomed, however, when the two girls worked out a sister act and opened at the Globe under the management of Salmon & Schuster. An interested member of the audience was Rufus Goldfish, who sat in the second roe (he was slightly hard of herring) and viewed the performance with a sardinic smile. "Confidentially," he told a grouper friends later, "the girls' act smelt, but they're pretty cute tricks. I found the one who was barracuda."

John Haddock's sole shriveled at these words. "Only an act of cod will keep my Bess out of his clutches," he muttered shadly. Mazie Angelfish tried to rally him. "Don't be blue," she counseled. "You are no common weakfish. You are a Haddock. Remember Dorothy Vernon of Haddock Hall. Get in there and put that bass, sailfish old flounder trout!"

John squared what passes for shoulders in a fish. "Thanks, Mazie," he spluttered. "By gum and bivalve, I'll get out of this pickerel yet. If that shrimp expects to mackerel have me to reckon with!"

Suiting the action to the words, he knocked his rival off his perch so effishently that poor Mr. Goldfish whaled for the carps—and a sturgeon to get the bones out of his mouth.

"I did it on porpoise," cried the exultant John Haddock, clasping Bess, who looked prettier than Marlin Dietrich, to his slippery chest.

It was all such a shark to Mr. Goldfish that he's been eel to this very day.

The Haddocks had a tarpon time of it ever after.

FINNY

Harold Cadmus, one of the big shots in the Scribner Press, was taking a few pleasant after-dinner puffs on his pipe in a train from Princeton to New York when an angry lady with a Pekinese dog under her arm descended upon him, yanked the pipe from his mouth, and threw it out of the window. Mr. Cadmus, always an impulsive gent, promptly seized the lady's Peke and threw that out too. By the time the train reached New Brunswick everybody in the car had joined in the ensuing argument. It ceased abruptly when down the track marched the Pekinese calmly smoking the pipe.

This is Mr. Cadmus's story, anyway.

"Madam," said the kennel owner to the *nouveau riche* sportswoman, "I offer you this thoroughbred bloodhound." "How do I know it's a bloodhound?" she asked doubtfully. "Hector," the owner ordered the dog, "bleed for the lady."

Aunt Jemima lumbered into a village depot clutching the hand of a pig-tailed little girl, and said, "One ticket fer Carolina." "What part of Carolina?" asked the station agent. "All of Carolina," said Aunt Jemima. "Dis am Carolina holdin' mah hand."

The Oppenheimer brothers were interviewing applicants for the job of private secretary. One Amazonian creature had excellent references, but the brothers did not enthuse after she waddled out. "I don't think she'll do," said one. "There's too much of her in the first place." His brother added, "That goes for the second place, too!"

George Abbott complains that play scripts are getting shoddier all the time. "The last one," he reports, "was so terrible, I had to rewrite the second act before I rejected it."

A fair customer of Goldstein's delicatessen marveled at his consistent perspicacity. "What makes you so smart?" she wondered. "Herring heads," said Goldstein promptly. "Eat enough herring heads and you'll be positively brilliant." "Can I buy some here?" she asked. "Certainly," said Goldstein. "They're fifty cents apiece."

The lady took three. A week later she complained that her I.Q. was unchanged: "You didn't eat enough yet," said Goldstein, so this time she took twenty herring heads. Cost: ten dollars.

On her next visit, she was more perturbed than ever. "Say," she accosted Goldstein. "You sell me a whole herring for fifteen cents. Why should I pay you fifty cents for just the head?" "You see," beamed Goldstein, "how much smarter you're getting?"

Bob Considine tells about a fight in a second-rate arena that failed to entertain the bloodthirsty spectators. The two contestants acted more like rhumba dancers than pugilists; they circled each other warily, exchanging practically no punches. After a deep silence, a voice rang out from the back: "Hit him now, yah big bum. Yah got the wind wit' yah!"

"Patrolman Cassidy calling," came a voice from the hall, accompanied by a loud knocking on the door of Apartment 6-B.

"What do you want?" a woman demanded from within. Her voice did not suggest rippling waters.

"It's your husband," hollered the cop. "A big steam roller just ran over him."

"Well, don't stand there talking," commanded the wife. "Slide him in under the door."

Among the many stories of how Mme. Du Barry first won the attention of her King, this one is as credible as any. Struck by her surpassing beauty, he summoned her to his side. The good lady had been planning this encounter for months, but she contrived a maidenly blush, and trembled visibly as she curtsied. "Are you accustomed to trembling in this manner?" said the King with a smile. Mme. Du Barry cast her eyes downward and replied softly, "Not before Your Majesty's enemies."

At the beginning of the nineteenth century, there lived in England a resourceful nobleman named Berkeley who traveled without guards, despite the prevalence of highway robbers. He declared that he was not fool enough to combat superior numbers, but that he never would surrender to a lone highwayman.

One night, on his way to London, his carriage was stopped by a man on horseback, who put his head in at the window and said "Lord Berkeley, I believe you have always boasted that you would never surrender to a single highwayman?" "I have," said Berkeley. "Well," said the stranger, producing a pistol, "I am a single highwayman, and I say, 'Your money or your life!'" "You cowardly dog," cried Berkeley, "do you think I cannot see your confederate skulking behind you?" The astonished highwayman looked hurriedly round, and Lord Berkeley promptly shot him through the head.

Another story of Lord Berkeley's ingenuity, and a clue to why he left a million pounds when he died, concerns the night he was entertaining a crony at a local tavern. As he was preparing to pay the bill, a guinea slipped out of his hand, and rolled into a deep crack in the uncarpeted floor. "I guess you'll have to count that guinea lost," said his companion. "Not at all," said Berkeley. He called the waitress, and said, "My dear, I've dropped two guineas. You'll find them here somewhere if you're patient. Now we are in a hurry, so if you'll give me one guinea now, you can keep the extra one for yourself when you find it." The transaction was completed, everybody was satisfied, and Lord Berkeley and his friend set out for the play.

Crosby Gaige, producer and epicure, sometimes drinks as many as eight varieties of wine with a full-course dinner. A friend once said, "I should think you'd be afraid of so many different wines at one meal." "I'm not," Gaige answered brightly. "It's only the indifferent wines I'm afraid of."

A few reasonably new stories about youngsters ("moppets," if you read *Time* magazine):

The first time a country kid saw a peacock at the Central Park aviary he exclaimed to his mother, "One of the chickens is in bloom." . . . . "Where is Cleveland?" asked the teacher. "Cleveland's in New York today," declared an alert student, "and Bob Feller is pitching!" . . . . "I guess you never heard of my home town," said a visitor. "It is called Timbuctoo." "Yes, I have," said the little daughter of the house. "Our church just sent a missionary there." . . . . "You bad boy," cried an exasperated mother.

"Didn't you promise you wouldn't bite your baby sister again?" The boy hung his head and explained, "I forgot not to." . . . . "I won't be able to join the gang tonight," apologized young Horace over the phone. "I promised Father I'd help him with my homework." . . . . Miss Dinglewasser, who presided over 6-A, returned to her pupils after an operation on her nose, and found the diplomat of the class waiting with a shiny, red apple. "Welcome back, teacher," he caroled. "You look a hundred years younger!" . . . . Warner Leroy, asked to name the Great Lakes, wrote in an examination paper, "Michigan, Erie, Ontario, Huron, Superior, and Veronica." . . . . "Hey, Pop," called little David, "Remember that dog you named Ben? It just had puppies, so I renamed it Ben Hur." . . . . Finally, a lad was instructed to use "archaic" in a sentence, and came up with "We can't eat archaic and have it, too."

Grandpa Cartmell was celebrating his 100th birthday and everybody complimented him on how athletic and well preserved he appeared. "I will tell you the secret of my success," he cackled. "My wife and I were married 75 years ago. On our wedding night we made a solemn pledge that whenever we had a fight, the one who was proved wrong would go out and take a walk. Gentlemen, I have been in the open air practically continuously for 75 years."

When Max Schuster, the publisher, bought a new home in Long Island, so many friends insisted that he install a croquet ground that the adamant Schuster had a sign printed, reading, "With mallets towards none." As an afterthought, he had a box built, marked,

"File and Forget Department. Guests are requested to drop all suggestions for altering the house and changing the grounds here." Incidentally, the box has no bottom; all suggestions fall directly into Long Island Sound.

Schuster met another eminent publisher, Charles Scribner, at a literary soirée. "Don't you think we know each other well enough to use first names?" he asked. "I do," agreed Scribner. Schuster extended his hand. "Hello, Charlie," he said. "Hello, Simon," answered Scribner.

Schuster recalls one fantastic day early in 1933 when every bank in the country was closed, and every bookstore was open. "Frankly," he says, "I never thought I'd live to see the day."

The mighty Simon and Schuster dynasty was founded in 1923, and became famous overnight when its crossword puzzle books swept the country. Another book on its first list was a biography of Joseph Pulitzer. Years later, somebody asked Max, "Wasn't that your first book to win a Pulitzer Prize?" "No," said Max, "but it was the first one that didn't have a pencil."

Ted Shane, one of the most brilliant of the humorists who began their careers as editors of the Columbia *Jester*, defines a husband as a sweetheart after the nerve has been killed. "Golf," he says, "is a game where a little white pill is chased by a lot of gaffers too old to chase anything else."

Ted once entered a restaurant and ordered six fresh oysters and six bad ones. "The bad ones," he explained, "are for my tapeworm."

He swears he knows a retired sea captain who buys

the *Times* every morning in New York, and then sends a little boy with it up to Yonkers, nine miles away, so he can read it by telescope.

Farmer Squibb was ploughing the farthest corner of his field when a neighbor came running to call, "Quick, Henry! Your wife's having a fit." Squibb dropped everything and ran a mile to his house. By the time he got there, his wife had recovered fully, and was placidly cooking dinner.

A week later he was summoned again. His wife was having another fit. This time he arrived, puffing and perspiring, to find his wife revived once more, darning stockings in the parlor.

A third time the neighbor called for Farmer Squibb. "Durndest fit she had yet," was the report. This time Squibb found his wife out cold on the kitchen floor. He felt her pulse and her heart. Neither stirred. He held a mirror before her mouth. There was no trace of moisture.

Farmer Squibb straightened himself and mopped his forehead. "Well," he declared, "this is more like it."

The conductor, making his rounds on the train, was surprised to find a little old man rolled up under one of the seats. Caught in his hideout, the little man pleaded, "I'm a poor old man and haven't got the money for a ticket. But my daughter is being married in another town, and I simply must get there for the wedding. Please let me stay here; I promise to be very quiet and not disturb any of the passengers." The conductor was a kindly man and agreed. But under the very next seat he found another little old gent huddled up and looking badly frightened. "And where are you going?" he asked. The man answered, "I'm the bridegroom."

Joseph Henry Jackson is the inventor of a game that calls for place names particularly suited to the states in which they are located. Examples: Shapeless, Mass.; Oola, La.; Goodness, Me.; Income, Tex.; Dathly, Ill.; Hittor, Miss.; Praise, Ala.; Coco, Colo.; Proan, Conn.; Farmerina, Del.; Inert, Mass.; Hezmakinizetme, Pa. This could go on indefinitely.

An English guide was showing Kenilworth Castle to some soldiers from the Bronx. "For hundreds of years," he proclaimed, "not a stone of this edifice has been touched, not a single thing repaired." "Say," observed one of the soldiers, "we must have the same landlords."

When Uncle Zeke got back to Tarleton Junction he swore he was through with New York for life. "I'm crossin' the street and mindin' my own business," he told his cronies round the old cracker barrel, "when a varmint comes lickety split around the corner on two wheels and knocks me flat. Do ye think he apologized? No siree! He leans out and hollers, 'Hey, Pop, as long as ye're down there, how about checkin' my oil?'"

Franklin P. Adams's son figures that the Ancient Mariner never could have made the big league. His fielding average was a lowly .333: "He stoppeth one of three."

When Benito Mussolini (remember him?) decided to go ahead with his invasion of Ethiopia, he selected his ten finest legions to spearhead the attack. Each legion consisted of 10,000 men. All of them were drawn up in the great Plaza in Rome while the Duce exhorted them from his balcony. "I know," he screamed, "that each one of my ten great divisions is going to fight for the honor of leading the attack. In fairness to everybody, I have decided to leave it to fate." He dramatically plucked a feather from his hat and threw it into the air. "Whichever man catches this feather," he announced, "will win for his division the glory of being the first to attack."

After this pronouncement, Mussolini went into his private office and waited for results. For a full hour nobody came near him. Mussolini, greatly perplexed, sneaked a look from the balcony window to see what was happening. The sight that met his gaze was 100,000 men, all puffing at the top of their lungs to keep the feather in the air.

A lunatic registered a terrific beef with his keeper. "You just don't treat Napoleon like this," he pointed out. "Yah," jeered the keeper. "Last week you told me you were Julius Caesar." "That," said the lunatic with great dignity, "was by my first wife."

A few weeks after Pearl Harbor, all Hollywood was repeating the story of the star who began worrying about her Japanese butler. She summoned him and quavered, "Hoshiro, after all these years in my employ, I hope you're not going to gumshoe in here while I'm asleep and slit my throat?" "No, miss," the Jap assured her. "Me no do thing like that. Gardener probably. Me just burn down the house.'

The following account, entitled "I Had Eighteen Bottles," is supposedly authentic. Even if it isn't, it has made the editors of eighteen joke books very happy:

I had eighteen bottles of whiskey in my cellar and was told by my wife to empty the contents of each and every bottle down the sink, or else. . . . I said I would and proceeded with the unpleasant task. I withdrew the cork from the first bottle and poured the contents down the sink with the exception of one glass which I drank. I extracted the cork from the second bottle and did likewise with it with the exception of one glass, which I drank. I then withdrew the cork from the third bottle and poured the whiskey down the sink which I drank. I pulled the cork from the fourth bottle down the sink and poured the bottle down the glass, which I drank. I pulled the bottle from the cork of the next and drank one sink out of it, and threw the rest down the glass. I pulled the sink out of the next glass and poured the cork down the bottle. Then I corked the sink with the glass, bottled the drink and drank the pour. When I had everything emptied, I steadied the house with one hand, counted the glasses, corks, bottles, and sinks with the other which were 29, and as the house came by, I counted them again, and finally had all the houses in one bottle, which I drank. I'm not under the afluence of incohol, as some tinkle peep I am. I'm not half as thunk as you might drink. I fool so feelish I don't know who is me, and the drunker I stand here the longer I get. Oh me! !

Chauncey Depew liked to tell the story of a young lady who tried to engage his services for a seduction suit against her employer. Depew told her she had insufficient facts to support such an action. She was very downcast when she left him, but returned triumphant the following morning, to report, "He seduced me again last night."

The maddening intricacies of English spelling are highlighted in this clever little poem, contributed to the publishers of Webster's Dictionary by Katherine Buxbaum of Iowa State Teachers College:

> I came beneath a pine tree bough
> When I was searching for my cough.
> I could not reach the pine cones, though,
> The branch was high and I was lough.
> "Ah, me," I cried, with rueful laugh,
> "Would that I were a tall giraugh."
> Just then a wind came hurtling through,
> The branches cracked, so fierce it blough.
> This blast, so shrill it made me cough,
> And on it went with angry sough;

I put my treasure in my mough
And started home across the slough
Forgetting what I'd come to dough.
Bossy was standing by her trough;
Did I mistake, or did she scough?

Readers who simply cannot stand Scotch jokes will escape five of them by skipping this paragraph:

... The one about the Aberdeenian who went behind the barn the night before Christmas, fired a shot, and then told his two children that Santa Claus had committed suicide.

... The one about the Edinburgher who whispered to one of the Siamese twins, "Get rid of your sister, an' I'll stand ye to a 'dr-r-rink.'"

... The one about the Glasgowleiter who emigrated to New York and was sitting on a pier in Jersey City when a diver came to the surface, removed his headgear, and lit a cigarette. "Hoot, mon," said the Scot, "why did no one tell me about this? I'd have walked over ma self."

. . . The one about the Glen Eaglet who wrote to an editor, "If you don't stop printing derogatory Scotch jokes, I'll stop borrowing your confounded magazine."

. . . And the one about the banker who left a thousand dollars each to an American, a Canadian, and a Scotchman with the sole proviso that each of them put ten dollars in his coffin to assure him first class passage in crossing the River Styx. The American and the Canadian each put in their ten-dollar bills. The Scotchman put in his check for thirty dollars and took out the two tens.

STOP!
DON'T READ
TOO MANY
JOKES AT ONE TIME.
THEY'RE FUNNIER IN SMALL DOSES

I was with Harry Ruby, the famous song writer and baseball fanatic, on just about the happiest day of his life last summer. Between games of a torrid Yankee-Tiger double-header, the Yank manager, Joe McCarthy (now replaced by Bill Dickey), told him he could don a New York uniform and work out the following afternoon with the "Bronx Bombers." "Just wait," boasted Harry, "till McCarthy finds out the only things I don't excel at are hitting, fielding, and running! But if he thinks he's gonna sign me up without a hefty bonus, he's nuts!"

Ruby has had his ups and downs in Hollywood. He didn't show up on one job for three years. "From the time I found out they don't like that sort of thing out there, it was easy sailing," he says. His favorite ballplayer (and he knows them all) is "Satchel" Paige, the perennial Negro pitching ace. "Satchel" was still slinging them in there on his fiftieth birthday. "How do you do it?" marveled Harry. "Easy enough," replied Paige. "I jest ain't never et anything at all what wasn't fried." After all, this was probably just as good an explanation as any.

As far as baseball managers are concerned, Ruby rates the late John McGraw, of the Giants, as master of them all. "When McGraw gave an order," he says, "it was either obeyed—or else. One day he sent a batter up to bunt. Instead the batter laid into the first pitch, hit it over the fence, and won the game for the Giants. The fans were cheering themselves hoarse as the player jogged into the dugout. McGraw looked at him with disgust and said, 'You're fired.' He was released the next day."

Heywood Broun was once introduced to a lecture audience by an old-fashioned local politician who sang his praises in broken-down clichés for a full twenty minutes. Broun finally arose, smiled, and said, "Ladies and gentlemen, now I know how a pancake feels when they pour syrup on it."

"Officer! Officer!" shrilled a lady on Sixty-second Street. "Come quickly! I've been robbed! Somebody broke into my house!"

The officer finished the banana he had lifted from Tony's fruit stand, and condescended to investigate. Then he turned to the lady with new respect. "Say," he said. "This is really serious. This window is busted on both sides!"

Early in Napoleon's career, he tested the valor of a newly enlisted corps by asking for volunteers to attack a strongly entrenched enemy position. One timid soul was shoved forward by malicious members of his squad, and before he knew exactly what was happening to him, found himself crawling alone in the night toward the enemy outpost. He came back unscratched and triumphant. "Sire," he reported. "I cut off the sentry's legs!" "Legs!" snorted Napoleon. "Why not his head?" "That wasn't possible," admitted the scout. "Somebody else had cut that off before I got there."

A soldier of fortune named Spectorsky joined the Foreign Legion and, to toughen him up, the head Shamus at Casablanca sent him on a thousand-mile solo trek through the Sahara Desert. The fourth day out, the valiant Spectorsky spied a wooden tower in the distance. For a while he thought it was a mirage, but no! As he drew closer, he saw that it was real. On top of the tower lolled a stoutish gent, reading *Variety*. He was dressed in a striped bathing suit with the word "Lifeguard" emblazoned across his manly chest.

"What are you doing 'lifeguarding' in the middle of the Sahara?" called Spectorsky in his best Riff dialect. "Don't you know it's at least a thousand miles to the nearest water?"

"Sure I know," said the lifeguard. "But isn't this one wonderful beach?"

Herbert Mayes, editor of *Good Housekeeping*, once turned down a short story by a very prominent lady writer, and she was petty peeved about it, too. She spied him at a cocktail party a few days later and began making a series of derogatory remarks. Mayes grinned knowingly and at a moment when everybody was listening remarked, "Don't look now, my dear, but your rejection slip is showing."

Mr. Pitkin was ailing so visibly that his friends persuaded him to go to Johns Hopkins for a checkup. The first doctor he spoke to said, "For your case history, I want you to give me a faithful and detailed account of a typical day's routine."

"Let's see," said Pitkin. "I get up about eight, wash, dress, eat breakfast, vomit, go to the office. . . ."

"Hold on!" cried the doctor. "Would you repeat what you said, please?"

"Okay," said Pitkin. "I get up at eight, wash, dress, eat breakfast, vomit, leave for the office. . . ."

"Do you mean to say," the doctor interrupted incredulously, "that you vomit every morning after breakfast?"

"Of course," said the mystified Pitkin. "Doesn't everybody?"

Frazer spent his first vacation in twenty years in the White Mountain. On the fourth day, his wife finally wheedled him into deserting the hotel lobby and going for a hike in the woods. He was back in an hour, his Brooks Brothers sports ensemble in tatters, and his face and arms bleeding from a dozen abrasions. "A snake chased me," he gasped, still terrified. "But darling," said Mrs. Frazer, "the snakes around here aren't poisonous." "So what?" barked Frazer. "As long as they can make me jump off a fifty-foot cliff, they don't have to be"

It was at the Atlantic City Beauty Parade. Miss Texas slithered by in her form-fitting white bathing suit. Grosvenor Maitland, Princeton '49, found his heart beating faster and declared, "Joe, this is love at first sight!" "Don't be silly," counseled his friend Joe. "It's just a passing fanny."

Mother Manges was pleased. "You see, Jerry," she beamed, "I told you that was a nice little boy next door. I was glad to see from the window just now that you had made friends with him and were helping him pick up his marbles."

"Marbles," scoffed Jerry. "I socked him in the jaw. Those weren't marbles; those were teeth!"

The famous theatrical partnership of George M. Cohan and Sam Harris furnished Lou Holtz with one of the prize stories in his repertoire. They were entertaining at Dinty Moore's one night, and the party kept growing and growing. So did the check. At closing time, Harris asked Dinty for the bill, but Cohan grabbed it away from him. "I warn you," said Harris to Moore, "that if you let Cohan pay this check, I'll never eat in this restaurant again." Cohan interrupted angrily, "And if you take one penny from Harris, you'll never see me in here either."

Faced with the loss of two of his best customers—not to mention the patronage attracted by their mere presence, Dinty Moore did some very quick thinking, swallowed hard, and declared bravely, "No more quibbling, gentlemen! This check is on the house." And he tore it into shreds.

As they left the restaurant, Cohan thumped his partner heartily on the back. "Well, Sam," he said. "The old act seems to be working as good as ever!"

Hal Block met a little cockney who enthused over a cruise he had made to South America. "First," he reported, "we stops in Cuba, and then we puts in at Haiti." "And what comes after Haiti?" asked Block politely. "H'eighty-one," said the cockney.

Heller and Son, Housepainters, was a partnership built on sand. The father was a meticulous, painstaking workman who believed in old-fashioned methods; the son was an impetuous, up-and-coming lad who liked to keep abreast of the newest developments. One day, the pair were painting a skyscraper, and were up to the forty-fifth floor. Suddenly the rope at the son's end of the scaffold gave way and the two men went cascading into space. The father passed the son at about the twenty-second floor, and just had time to scream as he whizzed by: "This will teach you and your darn boy-scout knots!"

Fred Allen dismisses Hollywood in the following short summary:

"Hollywood is a place where the girls have false hair, teeth, and calves on their legs. The men have their shoulders pulled up and wear toupees. When two stars make love on the screen, it's not two people making love; it's a lot of commodities getting together. California is all right if you're an orange."

Phil Baker adds that the state of California is going to keep all its antiaircraft guns in commission. They'll shoot down any rain clouds that come drifting in from Florida.

Baker also says he read that Christopher Columbus and his crew cruised around to see what they could find, and asks, "How is that different from modern sailors?"

(The last sailor I met was the captain of a Staten Island ferry boat, and his girl had just given him the air because he admitted he had a sweetheart in every port.)

Andy asked the new parlormaid, "Are ye fond of movin' pictures, Jeannie?" "Aye," said she readily. "Guid, lass. Then maybe you'll help me get half a dozen doon out o' the attic."

You've heard a lot about farmers' beautiful daughters, but Squire Parsons was one farmer who had a beautiful wife. When she went home to visit her mother, all the sunshine went out of his life, and when she wired him to meet her at the station on the 4:28, he hitched up his bay stallion in a fever of anticipation. The stallion had been cooped up in his stall for days and was rarin' to go. He wheeled into the turnpike at fifty an hour, and began picking up from there. Squire Parsons tugged in vain at the reins, and hollered "whoa" until his lungs almost gave out. Finally, as they thundered over Bear Creek Bridge, he cried out, "Hey, you gol' durned fool! Who do you think got that telegram, you or me!"

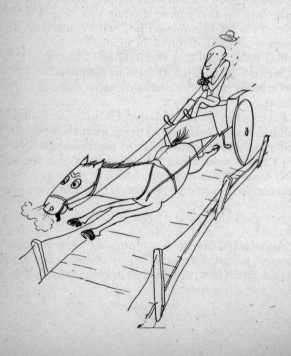

Rod MacLean, poet laureate of Los Angeles, submits a sheaf of four beautiful sentiments:

The groom wore black—white tie and tails—plus an air of manly pride. And like a lot of other males, he made a LOVELY bride.

All I know about a lynx is, confidentially, he slinks.

How sweet the way of a man with a maid! How touching the things he'll do! You'd think the guy was on a crusade. His wife treats the maid well, too.

Little Miss Muffett has so much stuff it makes her stick out in a crowd. Without hesitation I'd term her foundation the heaviest ever endowed. . . .

Rod was one of the guests at a Waldorf cocktail party in honor of the Duke and Duchess of Windsor. The Duchess presided graciously; MacLean whispered to a companion, "She never reigns, but she pours." (MacLean, inveterate punster, is also responsible for the use of the word "apocryphal" in the following sentence: "Hippety, hippety, hop, to the corner shop, for apocryphal of candy.")

Dick Lauterbach interviewed Shostakovitch in his Russian home. The famous composer was looking forward to a trip to America as a guest of Koussevitsky and the Boston Symphony, and in their thorough Russian way, he and his wife were studying English assiduously. The door had a sign on it marked "Door." The curtains were labeled "Curtains." Stalin's photograph, instead of his name, bore the inscription "Picture." And at Shostakovitch's table was a big placard that read, "I DEEPLY APPRECIATE YOUR MAGNIFICENT RECEPTION AND AM VERY SORRY I AM SO LATE."

Bernard Shaw stories number 6471 and 6472: He was eating his usual meatless dinner with a learned confrère when the restaurant's orchestra struck up a particularly noisy piece. When, after the briefest of intermissions, it launched into an even noisier one, Shaw summoned the headwaiter. "Does this orchestra play anything on request?" he asked. "Oh, yes, sir," said the headwaiter. "Excellent," snapped Shaw. "Kindly tell them to play dominoes."

An American met Shaw one morning on Piccadilly and stopped him with a "Say, are you Shaw?" "Positive," replied G.B.S.,—and walked on.

Jack Kapp of Decca Records has a very tony butler who has been picking up a nice piece of change on the stock market. When Decca's stock was hovering around 15 the butler asked Kapp how he liked it. "It's probably a good buy," admitted Kapp. "I agree," said the butler, "but I think I'll wait to pick it up when it reacts to 10." "If it ever reacts to 10," Kapp assured him, "you'll be out looking for a new job."

Fred Russell, sports editor of the Nashville *Banner*, tells about the time Coach Fritz Crisler was giving his boys a hot pep talk before the Yale game. He worked himself up to the point where not only the squad, but he himself was sobbing with emotion. "Now men," he begged with a broken voice, "go out on that field hallowed with the blood of your grandfathers and fight." The team went out to do or die and Crisler was well pleased with his performance until a lowly sub walked over and whacked him on the back. "Come on, Toots," he said sternly. "Get hold of yourself."

Another Russell classic: In the first round of a bout between two colored fighters, one was knocked flat, and the referee began to count over him. Observing that the boxer was in full possession of his faculties, although he lay motionless on the canvas, the referee didn't stop at "ten" but went cheerfully on with "eleven, twelve, thirteen, and fourteen." When he got clear up to "twenty-one" the fighter rolled over and said, "You is very fair, Mr. Ref, but I is through for the evening."

Two eyebrow-raising signs in the Boston Public Library: "No loose dogs allowed" and "Only low conversation permitted."

Henry Seidel Canby, author, editor, and Chairman of the Board of Judges of the Book-of-the-Month Club ever since that fabulously successful organization was founded in 1926, went to Australia last year to deliver a series of lectures on American literature. He came home with convincing tales of the effective part good books have played in spreading abroad a knowledge of the American scene and the American way of life.

One of his own books, however—his excellent biography of Thoreau—was the cause of a certain regrettable misfortune. Mr. Canby's Melbourne host thought so well of it that he insisted upon reading it aloud to his family. His oldest daughter, a senior in high school, listened carefully. Too carefully, perhaps. When the day came for her final examination in Geography, she confidently stated, "The three principal bodies of water in the United States are the Mississippi River, the Great Lakes—and Walden Pond."

From London comes the story of the pompous tycoon who was reading a prepared speech to a meeting of the nation's big shots.

"The average business man is tired," he thundered, pausing now and again to adjust his glasses. "He has worked twenty hours a day on war work, and more recently on reconversion problems. He is physically and mentally exhausted. But what a lead-pipe cinch he has had compared to the defenseless secretaries who have had to type all this interminable hogwash." The delighted audience let out a roar of laughter. The tycoon turned brick-red, gazed at his script in disbelief, and mumbled, "Extraordinary! I never wrote anything like that!"

Bob Hope, introducing a sally into literature called *Who Threw That Coconut*, by his fellow-thespian Jerry Colonna, explains, "There really are two sides to the Professor. One is the zany, silly moron. The other is the deep-thinking, serious moron. Jerry's really got a head on his shoulders—a triumph of plastic surgery."

Milton Berle is another famous comedian who has been dabbling in belles lettres. His compendium of wit bears the title, *Out of My Trunk*, and the story that the distinguished critic, Harry Hansen, singled out to quote in his review was the one about the interviewer who asked "Do you file your nails?" thereby giving Berle the opportunity to answer, "No, I just throw them away after I cut them."

You don't have to take it seriously, but Berle swears that he once drew pay as a lifeguard at Rockaway Beach. That episode in his career ended when a bather, going down for the third time, shrieked "Help! Help!" and Berle, on the shore, yelled back, "Swim in a little, mister. How do you expect me to throw a life preserver that far?"

Once Berle played Pittsburgh for a one-week stand. On Monday he picked out a restaurant that looked attractive to him, and liked everything except the bread. "I always eat whole wheat," he told the waitress, but she brought white. On Tuesday, he reminded her about the whole wheat, but was served white bread again. Wednesday she made the same mistake, not to mention Thursday and Friday. Finally on Saturday when she took his order, Berle said casually, "Just for the heck of it, I think I'll take white bread today." "That's funny," said the waitress. "Aren't you the party who always orders whole wheat?"

Eventually Berle reached Hollywood. They gave him a lawn party where all the glamour girls went to fantastic lengths to surpass one another. One wore three strands of genuine pearls, another wore a pendant that made the Hope Diamond look like something from Woolworth's, a third arrived in a Rolls with her Peke following separately in a Cadillac. One of the babes, however, showed the field up completely. She brought along her own swimming pool.

"You should see what that spendthrift Sadie bought at an auction sale today," reported Mrs. Ansbacher. "A Ming vase, no less!"

"Maybe," suggested her friend, "she wants it because it goes with her ming coat."

"Moonshine" McKeon, whose corn likker was guaranteed to knock out any West Virginian in three gulps, came charging into his cabin one day bristling with excitement. "Maw! Maw! Dang busted if I ain't larned to write." "What you larned to write, Paw?" said his wife. "Don't know, Maw," said Moonshine, a trifle deflated. "I ain't larned to read yet."

When old man Scott's lawyer learned that his client had inherited two million dollars and a five per cent interest in *Oklahoma*, he told his secretary, "I'll have to break it to him gently or the old coot will drop dead from the shock. Watch how I do it." They wheeled in the aged Mr. Scott promptly at three. "What's up?" he demanded crossly. "Mr. Scott," began the lawyer softly. "What would you say if I told you you had inherited a couple of million dollars?" Scott cackled, "Say? Why, Horace, you danged fool, I'd say 'Half of it goes to you.'"

The lawyer dropped dead.

An ambulance-chasing lawyer picked up a lady who had been knocked down by a Washington streetcar. "Here's my card, lady," he said, "I'll get you damages." "Don't be an idiot," snapped the lady as she dusted herself off. "I don't need no more damages. What I need now is repairs."

Arthur Szyk dined with two disconsolate Hungarians who deplored the sad state of the present-day world. "Things are so bad," sighed one, "that those who haven't been born yet are the really lucky ones."

"Ah, yes," agreed his friend, "but how many of them are there?"

Garfinkel was generally considered the most reliable and indefatigable millinery trimmings salesman in the country, but at long last his ceaseless pounding of the pavement affected his feet, and it was a very worried man indeed who presented himself to a foot specialist on Park Avenue. The specialist reassured him. "There is nothing intrinsically wrong with your feet, Garfinkel," he said. "I think you will be all right if you bathe them twice a day in salt water for a couple of weeks."

Garfinkel promptly went to Atlantic City, and secured a room at a hotel some three miles from the beach. The morning after his arrival he dragged his weary dogs down to the boardwalk, bought a big tin pail, and accosted a burly lifeguard nearby. "Would it be all right," asked Garfinkel, timidly, "if I took a pailful of your salt water?" "Sure," said the kindly lifeguard, "but it will cost you a quarter." Garfinkel dutifully produced the two bits, filled his pail with water, lugged it back to the hotel, and luxuriated in the first foot bath of his life.

Late that afternoon he reappeared at the beach with his empty pail. By this time the tide had gone out. The beach was fully 100 yards bigger than it had been in the morning. "Tsk, tsk," clucked Mr. Garfinkel, shaking his head. "Is that fellow doing a business today!"

Why is every absent-minded-professor story pinned on the brilliant but long-suffering Irwin Edman, the triple threat of the Columbia philosophy department? It definitely was *not* Irwin who was toying with a dissertation on Spinoza, and when his sister phoned to say "You must do something about the *Tribune*; it printed a story of your death this morning," answered, "Dear, dear! I suppose we must send flowers."

At the very last practice blackout in New York, former Mayor La Guardia was informed that the only thing that prevented a 100 per cent result was one little lightning bug who blithely ignored instructions. The mayor had the offender hauled before him and said, "Why didn't you observe blackout regulations?" "It's this way, Your Honor," said the lightning bug. "When ya gotta glow, ya gotta glow."

Haas and Klopfer became interested in modern art at about the same time. Haas bought a picture by an artist, whom the dealer assured him was the American El Greco, for two hundred dollars. A couple of weeks later he sold it to Klopfer for two hundred and fifty. Then Klopfer sold it back to Haas for three hundred. Gradually the boys worked the price up to a thousand. Then one day Klopfer reported that he had sold the picture to a rank outsider named Scherman. "You fool," chided Haas. "What did you do that for—just when both of us were making a fortune on it!"

Twenty or thirty years ago, all America was laughing at the exploits of Messrs. Potash and Perlmutter, inspired creations of the late Montague Glass.

There was the time, for instance, when Mawruss Perlmutter snagged the local sales agency for a dubious new automobile called the Schenkman Six, and promptly talked his old friend Abe Potash into buying the very first model that rolled off the assembly line.

Potash brought the car back the next day. "Mawruss," he reported, "about this Schenkman Six I got just three complaints to make. One: you gotta go into second to get over a manhole cover. Two: everything on the car makes a noise but the horn. And three: it may be sixty horse power like you say, but you forgot to tell me that all those sixty horses is already delivered to the glue factory. Incidentally, mein friend, that is where you go to collect your Schenkman Six."

Some months later Potash and Perlmutter decided to become motion-picture producers. The enterprising Perlmutter signed up a female star immediately, and exhausted his vocabulary describing her beauty and talents to his partner. Potash, as was his nature, remained unimpressed. "How much?" he inquired succinctly. "Well," said Perlmutter warily, "we gotta pay her six hundred dollars a week." "Six hundred a week," exploded Potash. "You want to bust us before we even begin?" "You don't understand," said Perlmutter. "This girl is a great bargain. She's a regular Kipling vampire." "Hmph," snorted Potash. "For six hundred a week she should kipple for somebody else."

Uncle Morris came home from seeing his favorite nephew off on the *Queen Mary* with his hair matted and his clothes in a dreadful mess. "There was a terrible crush at the dock," he explained. "Everybody pushing and shoving! Suddenly they started yelling, 'Man overboard!' I looked around—and my God, it was me!"

At Fifty-ninth Street and Fifth Avenue there stands a statue of General Sherman on horseback, being led by a gilded maiden representing Victory. A Southern matron looked at it and sniffed, "Just like the damn Yankees to let a lady walk."

It was an evil day for Tony when he cast in his lot with Pasquale. First Pasquale squandered every penny in their joint bank account. Then he sold the fruit stand right from under Tony's nose, and refused to pony up a penny of the proceeds. Finally Tony came home one night and found a note from his wife on the pincushion. It read, "So long, Tony. I have run away with Pasquale. No use trying to stop us. I love him." This was too much even for mild-mannered Tony. He shook his fist in the air and muttered darkly to himself, "Some day, Pasquale, you *gonna go too far.*"

At a luncheon of wives of Hollywood bigwigs, one producer's bride arrived literally dripping with diamonds. "Aren't they beautiful!" gasped a visitor from New York. "Hmph," snorted the hostess with a shrug, "lest year's jools."

A little later the New York lady had occasion to speak with the bejeweled matron. She came back with her eyes popping. "What do you think her husband made last year?" she whispered. "Half," snapped the hostess.

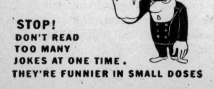

STOP!
DON'T READ
TOO MANY
JOKES AT ONE TIME.
THEY'RE FUNNIER IN SMALL DOSES

A FABLE that always gave me a chuckle concerned the Persian emperor who, while hunting, spied a very old man planting a walnut tree, and drew rein to ask him his age. The peasant said "I am four." When the emperor frowned, he added hastily, "I did not speak in jest, for the wise do not reckon the time they have squandered in folly; I therefore consider as my real age only the time I have spent serving my emperor and being a useful member of the community." The emperor, impressed, pointed out, "By your reckoning, you will never see those trees you are planting come to perfection." "True," agreed the sage, "but since others have planted that we may eat, it is only fair that we should plant for those who follow us." "Excellent," pronounced the emperor—and his approval in those days immediately called for a bonus of a thousand pieces of gold, which the old man was so pleased to receive that he bowed low and said, "Oh, King, other men's trees take forty years to come to perfection, but mine have produced fruit as soon as they were planted." "Bravo," said the monarch, and a second purse of gold was handed to the peasant. "What now," cried he. "The trees of others bear fruit only once a year, but mine have yielded two bountiful crops in a space of ten minutes." "Delightful," breathed the emperor, and a third purse of gold was turned over. At this point the emperor was heard whispering to his party, "Let us get out of this place fast or this witty old fellow will break the royal exchequer."

Babcock was intrigued by the advertisement of a canary that could sing every song in the world. What's more, the bird lived up to all his advance notices. On request, he warbled "Melancholy Baby," "Rule, Britannia," and an aria by Bach. "How much?" said Babcock. "Two hundred dollars," said the proprietor, "and you'll have to buy this other bird with him." "The two hundred is steep enough," complained Babcock. "Why must I buy this other bird as well?" "The canary needs him," said the proprietor. "That's his arranger."

The next time a visitor starts yapping to you about the "unbearable heat," you might try the response that Sidney Smith (a famous British reverend) used to shock a parishioner into silence. "Yes, it is very hot," he said. "Let us both take off our flesh and sit in the garden in our bones!"

One of Jack Benny's heftiest stooges confessed that his parents had hoped he would become a jockey. "You a jockey," gibed Benny. "Why, a jockey weighs only ninety-seven pounds." "That's right," agreed the stooge sadly. "That's what I weighed when I was born."

Practically any day now somebody is going to come along with a new plane that can get you from Grand Central Station to the Taj Mahal in an hour and a half, but it's still hazardous to fly from Newark to La Guardia Airport when there's no ceiling at one end or the other.

The theatrical sections chronicled the sad tale recently of a producer who was opening a show in Boston on a Monday evening, and discovered that morning that he was needed in New York for an urgent meeting. He boarded a plane, assuring his cast that he'd be back in Copley Square by mid-afternoon. Things didn't work out just that way, however. The airliner couldn't land in New York because of fog so it turned back to Boston. The fog had closed in there too by this time, so again there was no landing. Finally, the frantic producer set foot on solid land again—in Concord, New Hampshire! He hitchhiked to Boston, arriving almost in time for the second act.

When the reviews appeared the next morning, the producer was heard to murmur, "I should have stayed in Concord!"

Dixon Wecter tells about an elderly society leader of Charleston (than whom there really is nobody than whomer) who summoned a great-granddaughter to give an account of her fortnight in Paris. "The Louvre was wonderful," said the young lady, "and the biggest crowd always seemed to gather before the portrait of Whistler's mother." "I don't understand it," mused the beldame. "After all, she was only a MacNeill of North Carolina."

"I'm afraid my poor wife can never have a child," sighed a frustrated husband. "Inconceivable, eh?" asked a friend. "No, I mean unbearable," said the husband. "Impregnable," amended the friend.

A tony Park Avenue matron went to Cartier's to buy a solid gold drinking bowl for her prize Pomeranian. She toyed with the idea of adorning it with the inscription "For the Dog" in diamonds, but finally rejected it. "I guess it would be silly," she confided to the clerk. "After all, my husband never drinks water and the dog can't read."

Deacon Drearypuss was trying to impress an old sinner with the folly of betting on horse races. "Keep up your evil ways," he rumbled, "and you'll go to meet your Maker without a nickel to your name." "Ah, yes," sighed the sinner happily, "but what a way to die!"

Lapidus and his partner went fishing. The partner was lucky and pulled in a beauty. "Lapidus," he cried, "I tink I got me a haddock." From the other end of the boat Lapidus called back, "Vy don't you take an aspirin?"

The famous atheist, Col. Robert Ingersoll, owned a collection of curious and out-of-the-way books that was the talk of his community. One whole room was devoted to books on strange rites and ancient cults. "What do you figure this library cost you?" a visitor once asked. "Certainly the governorship of Illinois," answered Ingersoll, "and in all probability the presidency of the United States."

A three-year hitch in the Army enabled one observant recruit to boil everything down to three sacred rules. One: If it moves, salute it. Two: If it doesn't move, pick it up. Three: If it's too big to pick up, paint it.

The scientist who discovered the menace of bacteria in the gentle art of kissing back in the gay nineties provoked a characteristic outburst in William C. Brann, the fiery Texan editor of *The Iconoclast*. "Here in Texas," he thundered, "we take our kisses with the peeling or go without. We've got our hands full buttering up the maiden without bothering about the bacteria. Let those gloomy scientists with their double-geared microscopes croak what they may, the man who gets a chance to buss a corn-fed Texas beauty whose breath is sweet as that of a brindle calf fed on clover blooms doesn't have to give a damn for any fool bacilli."

Who knows but what it was young Mr. Brann himself who was riding in a day coach from Dallas to Austin when a frightened young man came dashing down the aisle with an enraged gentleman in full pursuit, crying, "Catch him! Catch the blank blank blank! Lemme at him! He offered my wife ten dollars to go off with him for the week end!"

Brann—if it was he—jumped from his seat, and joined the chase. He caught up with the fugitive in the baggage coach, and brought him down with a perfectly executed flying tackle. After the outraged husband had belabored his prostrate victim to his entire satisfaction, he turned suddenly to his accomplice and said, "How come, stranger, you were so anxious to help me catch this here maverick?" "I had a score of my own to settle," was the explanation. "I'll teach that so-and-so to raise the price o' romance in Texas!"

A sturdy Scotchman spent two years in a Nazi prison camp because he couldn't shake off his Aberdeen upbringing. He had escaped from his captors and was about to cross the Rhine in a rowboat when two Nazi officers appeared suddenly on the scene. Apparently they took him for a French boatman, for they indicated in sign language that they desired to be ferried across the river. The Scotchman obliged them, and they were halfway up the hill on the other side before he spoiled everything by hollering angrily after them, "Whisht, mon! Where's ma thr-r-ree and ninepence far-r-re?"

By this time probably one citizen out of every three in America has seen *Life with Father*. The play was tried out first in a summer theatre in a quaint old Maine town named Skowhegan. That was the year that they were building a new state highway. The official blueprints dictated that it be laid out right through the middle of the oldest cemetery in the vicinity. The natives grumbled a little bit, but respect for the law in those parts is very strong indeed and nobody did anything about it. In fact, several of the natives even got jobs working on the new road.

After one long rehearsal Howard Lindsay and Dorothy Stickney were having a cup of coffee at the lunch wagon on the main street when they heard one old boy say to a local member of the road gang, "You must be pretty well through the old cemetery by this time." "Yup," was the reply. "Have you reached my Great-Aunt Minnie's grave yet?" "Yup." "How was she lookin'?"

The road builder said, "Peak-ed."

There is a sawmill just outside of Skowhegan and a new worker was taken on one day. The foreman led him to a buzz saw, showed him how it worked, warned him that it was dangerous, and sauntered off. As soon as he was alone, the new workman, fascinated by the whirling contraption, reached an experimental finger toward it. One second later the finger was cut off. The poor workman let out a cry of pain and the foreman came rushing up. "What happened?" he cried. "Your darn saw cut off my finger," gasped the workman. "What in thunder did you do wrong?" cried the foreman. "Danged if I know," said the workman. "I just touched it like this—ouch, there goes another finger."

Remember those chocolate babies they used to sell in candy stores, ten for a cent? A little shaver demanded two cents' worth, and added, "I want all boy babies." The confectioner asked why. The little shaver explained succinctly, "More chocolate!"

A thirsty gentleman wandered into a corner saloon and ordered a dry Martini. He drank it with evident relish, and allowed as how it was the best darn Martini he ever had tasted in his life. "Do you always mix them this way?" he asked, "or was this one of those divine accidents?" The barkeep whipped up another one as proof, and the customer declared it was even better than the first one.

"Such genius deserves a reward," said the customer. He reached into his pocket and produced a live lobster which he pressed into the hands of the astonished barkeep. "Here! Take this with my compliments," he said.

The barkeep held the live crustacean gingerly at arm's length. "Thanks," he said dubiously. "I suppose I can take it home for dinner."

"No, no," objected the customer. "He's already had his dinner. Take him to a movie."

STOP!
DON'T READ
TOO MANY
JOKES AT ONE TIME.
THEY'RE FUNNIER IN SMALL DOSES

JACK COMINSKY, of the *Saturday Review*, once boasted of a system he had invented to preserve domestic well-being and tranquillity. "The day we were married, fifteen years ago," he said, "we decided that really important decisions were to be left to me. Small everyday decisions that affected only the smooth running of the house were left entirely to my wife." "How has your system worked out?" asked Amy Loveman. "Perfectly," said Cominsky. "There hasn't been a single hitch in the entire fifteen years. Of course," he added thoughtfully, "no really important decision has come up yet."

Horace Greeley had a long-standing feud with a rival New York editor. Said gentleman once boasted to a banquet audience, "Greeley had every advantage as a boy. I, on the other hand, am purely a self-made man." Greeley jumped to his feet and declared, "My worthy colleague has just relieved the Almighty of a terrific responsibility."

The editors of *The Reader's Digest* claim that each of the following five stories was submitted at least twenty times, in almost identical form, by people in every corner of the country.

1. Uncle Seth has a tactful way of telling evening visitors it's time to leave. As the town clock strikes nine, he says to his wife, "Come, Mama, we must go to bed so these folks can go home."

2. At a military funeral the aged mother of the deceased faints as the parting volley is fired. "My God," shouts the little boy. "They've shot Grandma."

3. A very generous tipper finds a brand-new waiter serving him one morning and inquires testily, "Where's my regular waiter Charlie?" Reply: "Boss, Charlie

ain't yo' reg'lar waiter no mo'! I done won you from him in a crap game last night."

4. A man in a bus or store absent-mindedly starts off with somebody else's umbrella, and returns it with abject apologies when the owner raises cain. Later in the day he buys three umbrellas at a bargain sale, and on the way home encounters the lady whose umbrella he had started to make off with in the morning. "I see," she remarks icily, "that you've done pretty well today."

5. A man orders steak and later is asked by the waiter, "How did you find your steak?" He answers, "I just lifted up one end of the potatoes and there it was."

Of course, the editors of The Reader's Digest know that most so-called "new" jokes are palpable rewrites of ones that were going the rounds a generation ago. People who are given to reading every new collection of funny stories published (we all have some kind of idiosyncrasy!) will come across the same basic jokes again and again. The Lord only knows who makes them up in the first place. The next time somebody accuses you of "stealing a joke" from him, just answer "Who told it to you?"

My son, Christopher, pulled his first joke on his fourth birthday. "What comes after seventy-five?" he demanded. "Seventy-six," I said indulgently. "That's the spirit," cried Chris, and rolled on the floor with laughter. He takes after his mother.

Fine thing happened at the Chrysler Building the other afternoon. A tenant whispered in an elevator girl's ear and she took him up on the twenty-second floor.

A vacationist from the city went fishing in a costume straight out of *Esquire*. A barefooted kid watched his ludicrous antics for some time and finally hazarded a "How many fish you caught, mister?" "None yet," said the mail-order Izaak Walton. "That ain't bad," said the kid. "Feller dressed even funnier'n you fished here for two weeks and didn't get any more than you got in half an hour!"

Riding in a dogcart, one wire-haired terrier said to the other, "Heard from your beau lately?" "Yes, indeed," was the reply. "I had a litter from him Tuesday."

Young Dr. Anderson hung out his shingle for the first time on a Tuesday, but no patient showed up until Friday morning. When one came into the room, Dr. Anderson thought it advisable to impress him. He picked up his telephone and barked into it, "I have so many patients scheduled to visit me today that I am afraid I won't be able to get over to the hospital to perform that brain operation until six this evening." He banged up the receiver and turned to his visitor with a disarming smile.

"What seems to be paining you, my good man?" he said. "Nothing is paining me," said the bewildered visitor. "I have just come to hook up your phone, sir."

When Dorothy Parker was reviewing books for *The New Yorker*, she dismissed one Pollyanna-ish novel as "perfect bathtub reading." "Just what do you mean by that?" demanded the indignant author. "I mean," said Mrs. Parker patiently, "that if I held the book under water, it would bob right up to the top. And if, at the end of my bath, the book went down the drain, that would be all right too."

Somebody ran across Mrs. Parker at the Viking Press offices last year and asked her what she was doing there. "Witting for my publisher again," said Mrs. P.

Another Parker story that was lost in the shuffle has reappeared. It concerns the time she was in a hospital recovering from a minor operation. There was a knock on her door and somebody asked, "May I come in?" Mrs. Parker answered, "Who goes there—friend or enema?"

Papa Slepperman was worried that his son might be forgetting his religion in the midst of the New York whirl so he wired him a reminder: "Yom Kippur starts tomorrow." Busy young Slepperman absent-mindedly dictated an answer: "Put a hundred on the nose for me."

Slepperman had trouble with his daughter, too. He sent her to an ultrafashionable girls' school and enrolled her in an extra-special ($500) class in etiquette. When Becky graduated, she plunged into society. One morning he found her crying hysterically. On the previous evening, it seems, she had attended a dance, met a very handsome and charming young man, and gone for a ride in the park that had disastrous results. "So," cried papa. "Who is this scoundrel, this wolf in ship's clothink? Tell me his name." When Becky shamefully admitted that she didn't even know his name, Mr. Slepperman's patience was at an end. "After all your lessons," he screamed, "you still not having the courtesy to esk, 'With whom am I having the plasure?' "

Russell Crouse recently divulged a couple of secrets about his incomparable press agent, Dick Maney. He took up the profession when an old hand at the game revealed how "easy" it was. "Press-agentry," he said, "is a gigantic hoax. If you have a hit, nothing you can do will keep it out of the papers. If you have a flop, you can hide diamond necklaces under each seat and no one will enter the theatre even to look for them. It is strictly a confidence game, but fortunately the Napoleonic code didn't get around to providing a penalty for it." Since that day, says Crouse, Maney has gone up and down Broadway like Robin Hood, stealing from the rich to give to the poor—Maney, in this case, being the poor. Crouse and Lindsay keep Maney in line by opening every conversation with him, "Maney, you're fired!" Billy Rose is another customer. In one of his dizzier flights, Maney referred to him as a "penthouse Cagliostro." "Who's that?" demanded Rose. "An eighteenth-century charlatan," soothed Maney. "Oh," said Rose, "a charlatan, eh? That's O.K.!" Maney is strong for week ends in the woods. He gets into his pajamas on Friday night and doesn't budge from the house until it's time to go back to work on Monday. "The country," he declares, "is beautiful. It's just the place to lick your wounds."

Al Shacht, the baseball comedian, insisted that his grandfather was major league timber too. "In fact," says Shacht, "he was the original brain trust of the Wahoo Woodpeckers. He always used his head. One day an opposing pitcher dusted him off at the plate. The ball conked Grandpa with a resounding crash, and turned into the most sensational home run on record. Yes, sir, it sailed over the right field fence, and won the game. The opposing pitcher committed suicide. They carried Grandpa off on their shoulders." "What nonsense," some literal-minded female usually exclaims at this point. "How could a man hit a ball over the fence with his head?" "You didn't know Grandpa," is Shacht's clincher. "He had bats in his belfry."

"A flash just came over the wire," a reporter told Ted Thackrey, editor of the New York *Post*. "There's been a violent earthquake in Pszczyna, Poland." Without looking up from the editorial he was writing, Thackrey said, "Find out the name of the place *before* the earthquake."

An impetuous young Williams student named Wimpfheimer negotiated a date with a pair of Siamese twins one night. "Have yourself a good time?" asked his awe-stricken roommate later. "Well," reported Wimpfheimer, "yes and no."

The census taker viewed Mandy and the six tots of varying ages around her with a puzzled frown. He seemed particularly intrigued with a squirming infant in her arms. "I don't quite understand you," he admitted. "Did you say that your husband died six years ago?" "Yes, sir," she replied emphatically. "He died, but I didn't."

Harry Kurnitz, witty scenario writer, and author of several first-rate mystery books under the pen name of Marco Page, escorted Florence Rice to a performance of *Die Walküre* at the Hollywood Bowl. All librettos

had been disposed of when they got there, and Miss
Rice confessed that she had never heard the opera
before. "Give me some idea of what it's about," she
requested. "Well," began Kurnitz. "The heroine is a
girl named Brünnhilde, who comes from a rather good
family. Her Father is God."

Mrs. Poore heard a crash in the kitchen. "More
dishes, Francesca?" she called with an air of resigna-
tion. "No, ma'am," came the voice of Francesca.
"Less."

The cashier of Taigue's Restaurant kept a paper napkin next to the cash box. "Whenever a customer walks off without his change," he explained, "I tap the counter with it as hard as I can."

Before the Nazis overran Southern France, a doughty old peasant woman had taught her parrot to say "*Mort aux Boches.*" A Gestapo agent heard the bird one morning and warned the old lady that the parrot would be killed, and she sent to a concentration camp if the parrot ever repeated the phrase. The old lady sought help from the village curé. He had a perfectly brought up parrot, he told her, and suggested a swap. The next day the Gestapo man, quivering with expectancy, glared at the bird, and grew choleric with rage when it said nothing. Finally the agent himself shouted "*Mort aux Boches.*" The parrot said softly, "May the good Lord answer your prayers, my son."

An eagle-eyed mortician noticed an old crone shuffling away from a funeral service at his parlor, and asked her how old she was. "One hundred and one," cackled the old lady proudly. "Well, well," said the mortician suavely. "Hardly worth going home, is it?"

The strong man of a one-ring country circus billed himself as "Hercules Junior," and was powerfully put out when he heard that a local farmer had boasted he could break Hercy in two. He took one of the big white horses from the ring and rode out to the farmer's house. "What kind of hooey have you been spreading about me, you runt?" he bellowed. The farmer didn't say a word. He just grabbed the intruder, hurled him bodily over the fence, and went back to his churning.

Hercules picked himself up, and gazed ruefully at the farmer. "Ain't you had enough?" called the latter, "or have you something more to say?" "No," admitted Hercules. "But maybe you'll be kind enough to throw me my horse."

"I think your husband is wearing a new kind of suit," said Rose. "Not at all," said Lily. "Well, he looks different," persisted Rose. "It's a new husband," explained Lily.

Joe Laurie, Jr., swears that he saw a traffic sign in a small Alabama town that read "No U-all Turns Here." He adds that the rules of etiquette were so strictly observed there that a man staring at a lot of shiny new dentures in a shop window was pinched for picking his teeth in public.

Once Joe dashed into a drugstore and cried "Quick! Give me ten cents worth of aspirin and some insect powder. I've got a lousy headache!" On the way home he caught a youngster prying the steps off an idle Fifth Avenue bus. The lad's explanation: "My father sent me out for some Carstair's but I figured bus stairs would do just as well." When friends had a baby daughter, Joe suggested that they word the announcement, "We have skirted the issue."

Everybody who loves Fanny Brice's inimitable portrayal of horrendous Baby Snooks knows about Baby

Brother Robespierre. A high spot in their career came
when Daddy received an offer of a thousand dollars a
pound for Robespierre from a childless couple. "Should
I sell?" he teased Baby Snooks. "How much does he
weigh?" she countered. "Thirty pounds," said Daddy.
"Let's keep the little stinker six months more," she proposed, "and fatten him up."

At the Hollywood Canteen one evening, Miss Brice
was thanked by a Marine for the swell poker chips she
had sent him. "Poker chips!" raged Miss Brice. "Those
were cookies." "That's as may be, ma'am," said the
Marine. "All I know is that last night I won eighty
bucks with 'em."

The foreman of a jury reported rather angrily to a
judge that no agreement on a verdict seemed in pros-
pect. "The jury will have to continue its deliberations,"
ruled the judge. "If you haven't come to a decision by
seven, I'll send in twelve suppers for you." "If Your
Honor doesn't mind," said the foreman, "I suggest that
the order be changed to eleven suppers and one bale
of hay."

"Shucks, Sunday school again," grumbled Willie.
"I bet Pop never went to Sunday school when he
was a kid." "He went regularly," his mother answered
him. "O.K.," agreed Willie reluctantly, "but I bet it
won't do me no good either."

A recent candidate for President of the United States
(he didn't make it) made an unexpected stop on his
transcontinental campaign tour, and his "ghosts" had
to whip up a speech for him in jig-time. He grabbed it,
stepped on to the observation platform, and began in

ringing tones: "Fellow citizens! It is an unexpected thrill to greet my friends in this typical American town, so rich in history and tradition. Slip in some corny joke here. . . ." The townspeople thought this was pretty funny, but friendly reporters agreed not to file the story.

❧

The *Zion Herald* front-paged the story of the city girl who was determined not to show her ignorance of farm life and manners. A Zion housewife put a dish of honey before her at the breakfast table. "Oh," she observed carelessly, "I see you keep a bee."

❧

An American tourist refused to be too greatly impressed with the masterpieces at the Louvre. "We've got plenty of priceless canvasses in the United States too," he declared. "I know," said his guide. "Rembrandt painted seven hundred pictures in his lifetime, and America has all ten thousand of them."

❧

Joe Frisco, the famous stuttering comedian, once found himself scheduled to appear on the same benefit program with the immortal Enrico Caruso. "What does he do?" Frisco whispered to a stagehand. "He is a singer," was the amazed reply. Frisco walked over to Caruso, tapped him on the shoulder, and stuttered, "Now l-l-look here, buddy, I am f-f-following you on this bill. L-l-lay off 'Darktown Strutters' Ball,' will you?"

There came a time when Joe Frisco had gone three full years without a single profitable engagement. One morning a big picture executive called and said, "Joe, I've got good news for you. There is a spot for you in one of our new pictures. It's yours for $200 a week."

"My salary," said Joe firmly, "is $2000 a week."

"Don't be arbitrary about this, Joe," advised the executive. "I suggest that you at least come down to my studio and talk the thing over with me."

"What?" cried Joe. "And get l-l-locked out of my hotel room?"

At a more lucrative period of Frisco's colorful career, he was summoned to the local income tax bureau and informed that he had made a slight miscalculation on his return. In fact, he owed the Government something like $60,000. The kindly souls gave him six months in which to pony up. On his way out of the office, Frisco discovered a young fellow Thespian waiting in the anteroom. "What do they w-w-want you for?" he asked. "It seems I've got to pay an additional $70 on my last year's tax," said the actor. "That's n-n-nothing at all," Frisco assured him. Then he turned to the federal investigator and said airily, "Just add that to m-m-my tab."

"What a change has come over your husband Zeke since we persuaded him to join the church," exulted a preacher in the hill-billy country. "Have you noticed it?"

"Sure have," agreed Zeke's wife. "Before, when he went visitin' on Sundays he carried his jug o' corn whiskey on his shoulders. Now he hides it under his coat."

Two street cleaners paused for a chat on Fifty-seventh Street. "What do you think of Ernest Hemingway?" asked the first. "Great stuff," said the second, "but don't you think he's a little too precious for the man in the street?"

From Bombay comes the story of the doughty old colonel, 74 or more, who startled the community by up and marrying a bouncing, beautiful girl of 19. A year later, furthermore, she presented him with a fine eight-pound son. The overjoyed colonel assembled the entire regiment, mounted the bandstand, cleared his throat, and announced, "I have called you all together to tell you that my wife gave birth this morning to a strapping baby boy. Gentlemen, I thank you."

A famous author was autographing copies of his new novel in a Cleveland department store. One gentleman pleased him by bringing up not only his new book for signature, but reprint editions of his two previous ones as well.

"My wife likes your stuff," he remarked rather apologetically, "so I thought I'd give her these signed copies for a birthday present." "A surprise, eh?" hazarded the author. "I'll say," agreed the customer. "She's expecting a Cadillac."

A patient in the hospital complained to Joe E. Lewis that he hadn't been able to eat a bite of food for four days. "You haven't missed a thing," Lewis consoled him. "It tastes the same as it always did."

In an idle moment, Joe composed the following couplet:

"Said a cigarette to the tray on the shelf,
I just go on making an ash of myself."

Incidentally, anybody who doesn't agree that Joe Lewis is the greatest night club entertainer in America can just go and dig these stories up somewhere else.

Ed Wynn is also a poet of note. If you don't believe it, study the nuances and subtle rhythms of his touching sonnet, "She Used to Go with the Landlord, but Now She Goes with the Lease."

There was a new watchman on duty at the Mt. Wilson Observatory, and he paused to watch a scientist gazing at the moon through the most powerful telescope. Suddenly a shooting star flashed through the heavens. The watchman dropped his pipe and exclaimed, "Man alive! What a shot!"

STOP!
DON'T READ
TOO MANY
JOKES AT ONE TIME.
THEY'RE FUNNIER IN SMALL DOSES

ONE OF the favorite stories of Abe Burrows, the radio and song writer, concerns the day he was riding in a car in New Jersey with a nervous playwright. The driver was reckless and erratic and had his passengers on the edge of their seats; when the towers of the George Washington Bridge loomed in the distance, the playwright tapped the driver on the shoulder and suggested, "Don't cross that bridge until you get to it."

That calls to mind the Earl Wilson story of the time Beatrice Lillie offered a lift to an actor she loathed. In her sweetest manner she asked, "Can I drop you anywhere—off the George Washington Bridge, for instance?"

One of the last of the Hatfields came down from the hills and sought a doctor. "Better come and look at my son-in-law," he said tersely. "He ain't been doin' so good since I shot him Tuesday." "That beats the Dutch," said the medico. "I always knew you Hatfields was quick on the trigger, but this is the first time I ever heard of one of you shootin' a member of his own family." Hatfield looked very hurt. "Believe me, doc," he said. "When I shot him he wusn't!"

That male shopper that was bounced out of Gimbel's toy department just didn't know where to stop his experiments. He squeezed one doll until it hollered "mama." Then he squeezed another one and she yelled "floorwalker."

The Halloran Military Hospital humorous department exhumed the venerable fable of the waitress who stood wondering why an elderly man plowed through a heavy dinner while his wife sat drumming on the tablecloth and gazing out of the window. "Aren't you hungry?" she asked the wife finally. "You bet I am," said the wife, "but I gotta wait till Pa's finished with the teeth."

Until recently Mr. Winston Churchill had a son-in-law whom he simply could not abide. The young man, an actor by profession, was acutely aware of the situation, and never ceased trying to correct it. His efforts got him nowhere. At one large formal dinner, for instance, at Chequers, the Churchill country estate, he suddenly remarked, apropos of nothing, "Sir, who do you think will go down in history as the greatest statesman of his age?" "Mussolini," said Mr. Churchill, without hesitation. Everybody was startled, of course, and the young man gasped "No! You can't mean that! Why Mussolini?" "It is very simple," said Mr. Churchill, puffing placidly on his cigar. "He is the only one of us who had sense enough to shoot his son-in-law."

Alfred McTichnor shook his head. "No, sir," he said, "I cannot accept your offer of a cocktail at this hour for three reasons. First: I promised my wife never to drink during the business day. Second: liquor before lunch incapacitates me for work all afternoon. Third: I had three just before you came in."

"However," continued McTichnor hurriedly, "I do not want to injure the feelings of a distinguished New York colleague. You might order me two double Martinis."

Walter Johnson, one of the greatest stars in baseball history, was asked how he pitched to Ty Cobb. "I used to give him the best I had," reminisced Johnson, "and then I ran over to back up third base."

The editor of this collection has always been a pushover for the humor of George S. Kaufman, and would not consider a book of funny stories complete without a few specimens of one of the sharpest and most telling wits of our time.

He and Max Gordon needed a girl with a powerful voice for a new musical, and he journeyed up to Carnegie Hall to hear a highly touted newcomer. "How was she?" asked Gordon eagerly that evening. "Terrific," said George. "She got such an ovation when she sang 'Ave Maria' that she encored with 'Ave Another Maria.'"

Watching Billy Rose play a hand of gin, George disapproved of the strategy—too, too understandable if you've ever seen Billy play gin. When his opponent schneidered him, George asked him, "Exactly what game did you think you were playing, Billy?" Rose, slightly nettled, answered, "I guess you'd call it only part gin." Kaufman added, "And part chesi."

"Age," he confesses, "has taught me patience in waiting for reviews of my new plays. Time was when I always sat up after an opening and waited for the morning papers. I would even sit up for *Time* and *Newsweek*, and once, I think, I sat up for Burns Mantle's *Year Book*. But nowadays I just go home and go to bed. You can be panned just as well in the morning."

In a recent musical Kaufman gave Victor Moore a line that seems to me to catch in one short phrase all the pomposity and pretentiousness of a typical business big shot with seven or eight telephones and an inter-

office buzzer system on his desk. Moore portrayed the role of head of a colossal motion-picture studio. Just before he went into a story conference, he picked up one of his phones and directed the operator, "Don't ring me unless there is somebody on the phone."

President Truman likes to reminisce every now and then about his brief experience in the haberdashery business. He remembers one very tough customer who was in the market for some shirts. Mr. Truman pulled out his most expensive line and said, "These wear like iron. They just laugh at the laundry." "Yes, I know," said the customer, unimpressed. "I have some just like these. They came back with their sides split."

The clerk at the Housatonic Bookshop told a Hotchkiss student, "Here's a book that will do half your work for you." "Great," said the student. "Give me two of them."

Little Willie tugged at his mother's apron strings. "Ma, didn't I hear you tell Aunt Mary I have your eyes and daddy's nose?" "Yes, you did," said his mother indulgently. "Well, look at me now ma," said Willie. "I got Grandpa's teeth."

Ginsberg had a remarkable run of luck in a dice game one day and piled up $3000 in winnings. He went to the well once too often, however, shot the whole $3000, and lost. The shock was so great that he promptly died of heart failure. His friend Solomon was designated to break the sad tidings to Mrs. Ginsberg. He found her baking a strudel in the kitchen.

"Your husband was in a little crap game this afternoon, Mrs. Ginsberg," he said diffidently by way of a start.

"The loafer," said Mrs. Ginsberg, continuing with her baking.

"He was ahead $3000," continued Solomon, "but he bet it all at one time and got cleaned out."

"$3000!" screamed Mrs. Ginsberg, now thoroughly aroused. "He should drop dead."

Solomon nodded gravely. "He did. Good day, Mrs. Ginsberg."

A Brazilian legend concerns a jaguar who persuaded a cat to teach him how to jump. After a few successful experiments with bugs and insects, the jaguar decided to try out his new technique on the cat itself. The cat, however, jumped out of danger like a flash, and the jaguar landed in a heap. "That isn't fair," whined the jaguar. "You didn't teach me that trick." "A smart teacher," the cat reminded him, "never teaches a pupil *all* his tricks."

A Hollywood ham, witness in an accident case, described himself as "the greatest actor since Booth." "Modest, aren't you," laughed the judge. "Ordinarily, yes," said the ham without blinking an eye, "but please remember that I am now under oath."

Three bulls escaped from a slaughter house. One was a big bull, one was a medium-sized bull, and one was a very small bull. The big bull ran into a barn across the road and was captured in no time flat. The medium-sized bull stopped for a red light on the corner and was promptly lassoed. The small bull, however, led his pursuers a merry chase before he was rounded up. The reason for this is that a little bull goes a long way.

Eddie Davis recalls that in his tenderfoot days he had an older partner who didn't quite understand what fifty-fifty meant. "In fact," says Davis, "he was so crooked that the wool he pulled over my eyes was 50 per cent cotton."

Appearing at his club one evening with a black eye, Davis offered a novel explanation: "A character with a build like Joe Louis told me I was Number One in his Hit Parade. Then he hit me."

A professional cardsharp spent a day at the race track and lost every nickel he had in the world. "Before I come out here again," he told himself, "I'm going to learn how to shuffle horses."

A man who was driving across the continent put up for the night at a rural hostelry. The view from his second-story window was lovely, he thought—peaceful meadows and a beautifully kept lawn directly below.

During the night, however, there was a cloudburst, and when the man awoke, the ground had disappeared under water fully five feet high. This was surprising enough, but then the man spotted something even more unusual. A straw hat floated by, reached the boundary fence, turned around, and floated back! Three times this phenomenon was repeated, and the man rushed to the proprietor with a hushed, "Do you see what I see?"

"Sure," laughed the proprietor. "That's Uncle Henry. Stubborn old coot! He swore he was goin' to mow that lawn this morning, come hell or high water!"

Two peddlers of children's dresses met on Second Avenue. "I don't understand how you manage to undersell me," said one candidly, "since I steal the materials from which I make my dresses." "You're a fool," said his friend with an equal burst of honesty. "Why not do like me? I steal the finished articles!"

At the opening performance of Sheridan's *School for Scandal*, the playwright noted with mounting anger that a rival in a stage box failed to crack a smile during the entire performance. In complaining about it later, he told a group of friends, "Cumberland was not only rude, but damned ungrateful. He had a tragedy open last Monday, and curse me if I didn't laugh my head off very loudly all the way through it!"

On the eve of March 15th Groucho Marx informed his brother Chico, "The time has come to talk of taxes."

"My friend Ravelli lives there," said Chico.

"No, no," corrected Groucho. "Not Texas. Taxes. The dollars we have to pay the government."

"Datsa what I said," insisted Chico. "Dallas, Texas."

Evidently tax hurdles were negotiated successfully, because we next find Groucho doing a graceful minuet with a beautiful débutante, and whispering softly, "This calls for champagne. What brand do you fancy?"

"Mumms '29," said the girl. "I am not interested in your mother's age," Groucho reminded her angrily. "I asked you what brand of champagne you wanted."

They have a lot of trouble translating some of Groucho's topical quips for the foreign versions of his motion pictures. In Go West, for instance, he met a formidable Indian and inquired, "Are you the chief who goes from Chicago to Los Angeles in 39 hours?" Obviously a movie fan in Stockholm or Rio de Janeiro wouldn't make much sense out of that. So a specialist at MGM had to rewrite the line for foreign consumption to read, "You must be the Indian who scalped my grandfather. That looks like his hair you're wearing for a toupee." They laughed in Rio, anyhow.

My idea of heaven: a new dramatization of The Three Musketeers, starring Groucho Marx, Bobby Clark, and Fred Allen.

A little pickaninny came running to a fat old lady who was rocking herself on the cabin porch and cried, "Mama, you can strike me down if I ain't just seen a big alligator down in the swamp with little Sambo in his mouth." The old lady continued her rocking and called out, "Ain't I been tellin' you, Ef, that sumfin' has been ketchin' them chillun?"

At a stag dinner in the Lambs Club, a group of well-lubricated convivials were startled by the sudden entrance of a weird character with flaming red hair standing on end, a chalk-white face, and a costume that looked as though it had been laid away in moth balls for a decade or two. Ring Lardner recovered first. He rose from his chair with some difficulty, and poking a shaky and accusing finger in the newcomer's face, demanded, "On the level, mister, how do you look when I'm sober?"

STOP!
DON'T READ
TOO MANY
JOKES AT ONE TIME.
THEY'RE FUNNIER IN SMALL DOSES

She sat on the bridge in the gloaming
And tickled his face with her toes.
But she was a Jersey mosquito
And the bridge was the bridge of his nose.

No joke book is complete without at least one Abraham Lincoln joke. Here it is. Young Abe took a sack of grain to a mill whose proprietor was known as the laziest soul in Illinois. After watching the miller at work for a while, Abe commented drily, "I can eat that grain as fast as you're grinding it." "Indeed," grunted the miller. "And how long do you think you can keep that up?" "Until I starve to death," said Lincoln.

An $8,000 limousine shot by a jalopy on a country road. The driver leaned out and hollered "Hey, rube! What's making that awful rattle in that chariot of yours?" "I reckon," answered the owner of the jalopy, "it must be the $7,500 jingling in my pocket."

"I don't get it," said one pretty girl as she divested herself of her undergarments. "I tell the doctor my sinus is bothering me and he asks me to strip." A naked redhead with a satchel on her lap replied, "My case is even more puzzling. I'm here to tune the piano."

A publicity-mad bobby-soxer thought she could land herself on the front page by grabbing Van Johnson as he got off a train and handcuffing herself to him. Unfortunately she made a slight error and slipped the

manacles on the wrist of the wrong man—a Mr. Henry
Schnitzman, of Red Bank, New Jersey. Furthermore,
it developed that she had lost the key and couldn't
unshackle herself. At last reports, Mr. Schnitzman was
sailing out of Penn Station in a high dudgeon, bound
for the police station, with the humiliated maiden dragging behind him, enchained and in tears. Informed of
the excitement, Van Johnson said with deep feeling,
"I hope he beat her ears off."

Samuel Hopkins Adams' biography of Woollcott is
a fascinating job. One story he overlooked, however,
concerned a chance encounter in Atlantic City between Mr. W. and Moss Hart. "You seem very chipper
today," observed Moss. "I feel like God," Woollcott
assured him. "Alec," said Hart sharply, "how often have
I told you to finish your sentences!"

"By you is trouble, Mrs. Kugel?" inquired a friend.
"You look terrible!"

"Yah, yah," sighed Mrs. Kugel. "Mein husband
Mosha is always sick."

"Mosha is just a hypercondit," said her friend. "He
ain't sick. He just thinks he's sick. Ignore his complaints
and watch him get well."

The two met again a month later. Mrs. Kugel looked
even more woebegone.

"Mosha is no better?" asked the friend.

"Worse," said Mrs. Kugel. "He thinks he's dead."

Otis Moore of Kenilworth, N.J., has been doing some
research on the subject of mules and sends me the
following out of a clear blue sky:

You know that Missouri stands at the head in raising mules? Because that is the only safe place to stand.

Ever hear of the mule skinner whose critter wouldn't move a step? He went to a vet to get something to give the mule. A half hour later he was back demanding, "Gimme a double dose of that stuff. I gotta catch that mule."

There is another hoary tale of a sick mule. The horse doctor prescribed a horse medicine to be blown through a tube into the mule's mouth. Soon the man returned looking mighty sick. "What on earth has happened to you?" asked the vet anxiously. The man replied, "That damn mule blew first."

"She laughed when I sat down to play," reported the inveterate ad reader, "but how was I to know she was ticklish?"

"So you like my pooch," beamed the sportily attired gent. "I'm glad. It cost a thousand dollars. Very rare breed. Part schnauzer. Part bull."

"Amazing," clucked the lady he had just met. "Which part is bull?"

The gent broke down. "The part about the thousand dollars," he confided.

A famous producer bought a ranch that he proposed to use as a haven to get away from it all. His wife, however, had different ideas and invited at least thirty people down for every week end. The producer walked in on one typical brawl and heard his wife bemoaning the fact that she hadn't yet thought of an appropriate name for the ranch. He looked over the assemblage of guests with distaste and cried, "I've got it. 'Bar None.' "

It was reported that when Mrs. Pat Campbell visited here she was asked to write something in the guest book. She scrawled, "Quoth the raven," signed her name, and departed.

An Englishman, a Welshman, and a Scot were having drinks together. There were three flies buzzing around the room, and one happened to light in each drink. The Englishman called for a teaspoon and removed his fly with an expression of disgust. The Welshman put his hand in and with his thumb and forefinger flipped his fly clear across the room. The Scot carefully lifted his fly and wrung it out.

In Kennebunkport, the late Booth Tarkington was asked via long-distance telephone to act as master of ceremonies at the burial services of a deceased bigwig. "Where is he going to be buried?" he inquired. "He is going to be cremated," was the answer. "You don't want a master of ceremonies," decided Tarkington. "You want a toastmaster."

The following little poem is very popular in Wisconsin and Minnesota, where the main body of Sioux Indians dwelled before the white men came:

> There once were some people called Sioux
> Who spent most of their time making Shioux
> Which they colored in various hioux.
> Don't think that they made them to ioux;
> No, no! They just sold them for bioux.

Irving Hoffman writes a daily column and does the drama reviews for the *Hollywood Reporter*. On the side he makes a modest fortune as a publicity counsel. Nobody knows the names of his clients but everybody knows they're important.

Hoffman is the most nearsighted man in New York. He identifies pretty girls (and he knows them all!) by the Braille, or touch, system. Pamela Drake says he is so near-sighted that when he can't sleep nights he has to count elephants.

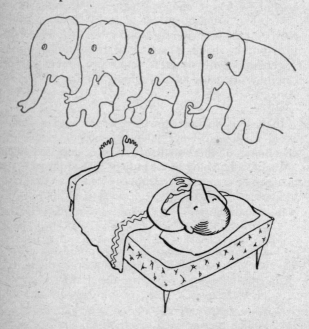

His drama reviews lean a trifle too much to the wise-crack school, but in a period when good critics can be counted on the fingers of one hand, his devastating brush-offs have become legendary, and are picked up regularly by other columnists, *Time*, and digest magazines. Of *Mr. Strauss Goes to Boston*, he noted, "This was one book Boston was really entitled to ban." "*Good Night Ladies*," he said, "is one of those turkeys that hopes to get by with very little dressing." He described one buxom starlet as "a girl who probably takes Wheaties for breakfast every morning, and talks on the stage as though her mouth were still full of them." *A Lady Says Yes* was dismissed as "mad doggerel where the music is tin-pan and the humor is bed-pan. The leading lady, a pip who used to zip and strip, now just stands around and twiddles her tum." In *Marinka*, "the only distinguished thing about the music was its ancestry. Every once in a while the chorus broke out into an Albertina Rasch." When Hoffman likes something, however, he goes to equal lengths to help put it over.

One of the Tales of Hoffman cites the enrollment of Shirley Temple at the age of five in a kindergarten whose other pupils were seven. "Shirley is precocious," Mrs. Temple assured the teacher. "Say some words," said the skeptical teacher to Shirley. "Purely irrelevant words?" asked Miss Temple, "or would you prefer me to shock the hell out of you?"

Mrs. Temple said later that her decision to enter Shirley in school had been based not only on the child's obvious aptitude, but on the advice of a visiting educator. "How early do you think I should begin my child's education?" Mrs. Temple had asked. "When will it be born?" he countered. "Born?" gasped Mrs. Temple. "Why, she's already five years old." The educator said sharply, "Don't stand here talking to me then! Hurry home—you've already lost the best five years!"

A drunk in a nightclub wanted to go to the washroom. The barkeep handed him a big key and warned "Don't forget to lock it when you come out." In due course the drunk solemnly returned the key and delivered this discourse. "My grandfather had a million dollars and six bathrooms. My father had five million dollars and ten bathrooms. I have twenty million dollars and two dozen bathrooms. Not one of those bathrooms ever had a lock on it. And would you believe it, mister, neither my grandfather, my father, or myself ever *lost a thing*."

Byron Nelson is the kingpin of the golf world today, but oldsters say he has nothing on Harry Vardon when it comes to accuracy. "Vardon had only one weakness," reports Fred Corcoran. "He couldn't play thirty-six holes in one day over the same course. That bird was so accurate that on the second round his ball would invariably land in his own divot."

Gottfried, of the Madison Avenue Gottfrieds, turned pale when his brother walked into the store. "What's happened?" he gasped. "Don't be frightened," said his brother. "I just fell asleep in the chair and Grecco, the barber, cut my hair a little too close." "Hallelujah," said Gottfried with a sigh of relief. "I thought the Indians were on the warpath again."

A motorcycle cop stopped a car and pulled out his summons book. "I clocked you at forty-five, mister," he said. The lady in the back seat cackled gleefully. "Just you give him a ticket, officer. Serves him right. I've told him for years he's a reckless, inconsiderate, dangerous driver!" "Your wife?" queried the cop, and when the driver nodded glumly, he snapped the summons book shut and added, "Drive on, brother."

"How did Wartel get such a cast in his eye?" asked a bookseller. "I hear," confided the jobber, "that he took his wife fishing last winter."

Ted Cott sings the praises of an amateur symphony orchestra in Duluth, the city adopted by Sinclair Lewis. One of the mainstays of the organization is an obstetrician, and he can produce golden notes and seven-pound twins within a single hour without mussing a hair on his head.

Dolled up in dinner clothes for a scheduled concert one evening, the good doctor was summoned for a special delivery. The mother-to-be saw him enter in his glad rags, smiled feebly, and said, "Why, Doctor! I didn't know this was going to be formal."

They still are telling stories about One-Eye Connolly, the greatest gate crasher in history. Chided for letting "One-Eye" slip past him at a heavyweight championship bout, a ticket taker explained mournfully, "That bird walked in backwards so smoothly that I thought he was coming out!"

The St. Louis Medical Society Bulletin clears up everything with this bit of scientific research:

When Nature first created man, monkey, and bull, she endowed the man with forty years of life, the monkey with forty, and the bull with twenty. The man wanted more, and the monkey and the bull volunteered to help him out. "Twenty's enough for me," said the monk. "Man can have my other twenty." "And I'll give him ten of mine," said the bull.

And thus it came about that man's life runs to seventy years on the average, and is divided into these three periods: first forty years, normal living; next twenty, monkey business; last ten, shooting the bull.

Advertisement submitted for the Classified column in the *Saturday Review of Literature*:

"Will the person who stole the jar of alcohol from Room 308 in the Cornell Medical Center kindly return my aunt's appendix? No questions asked."

Joe Besser boasted that he owned an antique bed that "both George Washington and Napoleon slept in." "Now how on earth could those two men possibly have slept in one bed?" asked one skeptic. "Don't be stupid," said Besser. "It was a double bed."

"Pay some attention to mama," a pretty girl demanded of her swain. Put on the spot, the young man cleared his throat and said with an ingratiating smile, "Mrs. Jones, the last time I saw a mouth like yours, there was a fishhook in it."

The very orthodox Mr. Shlepkin was so outraged to discover his rabbi coming out of a subway station on a Saturday morning that he seized a harmonica and dogged the footsteps of the mortified rabbi for four blocks playing "Onward Christian Soldiers."

Harold Hart has gathered a bouquet of poison-ivy sprigs hurled at women by some nasty old cynics who probably never had a girl of their own with great big beautiful blue eyes. Samuel Butler remarked, "Brigands demand your money or your life. Women require both." H. L. Mencken declared, "Thirty is a nice age for a woman—especially if she happens to be forty." That meanie Herb Swope pointed out that a woman who is always up in the air and harping on something is not necessarily an angel. "Women are like socks, and should be changed frequently" is attributed to John Lewis French. And could it really have been John Barrymore who counseled, "The way to fight a woman is with your hat. Grab it and run"?

The barkeep of a downtown tavern kept a pet parrot. One evening a drunk spotted it, climbed atop a stool, and tried to catch hold of it. "Scram, landlubber," shrieked the outraged pol. "What's the big idea?"

The drunk looked surprised, tipped his hat, and mumbled, "Golly, I'm sorry, mister! I thought you was a boid!"

Vittorio was a very smart little boy, not particularly addicted to taking baths. Things reached a point where his schoolmates shied away from him, and his teacher, who liked to see him high in his class, but not too high, sent him home with a note to his mother. It read, "Your Vittorio is a fine boy, but he doesn't smell so good. Won't you please see that he bathes more regularly?" Back to the teacher came Vittorio with a communiqué from his ma. "My Vittorio," she pointed out, "ain't no rose. Learn him, don't smell him."

In a tight-fisted Iowa congregation, the hat was passed round one Sunday and returned absolutely empty. The pastor cast his eyes heavenward and said reverently, "I thank Thee, oh Lord, that I got my hat back."

Jack Kirkwood, boasting of his prowess as an ice-skater, told how he had mastered the art of cutting figure eights. "It's the simplest thing on ice," said the sponsor. "Not the way I do it," retorted Kirkwood. "I make five with one foot and three with the other."

"Why are you staring at me so?" a man seated in a subway train protested to a fellow swaying on a strap in front of him. "I'm sorry," was the reply, "but you know, if it weren't for the mustache, you'd be a dead ringer for my wife." "Mustache?" queried the one who was seated. "You must be nuts. I have no mustache." "No," agreed the other. "But my wife has."

At a Dutch Treat Club luncheon Edmund Gwenn told the story of the day John Drew ordered kidneys for lunch at the Players, and then repaired to the bar for a couple of snifters with the boys. A half hour later, a waiter whispered discreetly to Drew, "I don't want to disturb you, Sir, but your kidneys are spoiling." Drew answered, "I've suspected that for years, but didn't realize it was visible to the naked eye."

Mr. Heimerdinger was interviewing applicants to replace his private secretary who had resigned because of expectant motherhood. His assistant sat with him while he looked the young ladies over.

The first applicant was a luscious, blue-eyed blonde. The second was a photogenic redhead who looked like a Hollywood starlet. The third one was cross-eyed, single-toothed, and weighed about 240 pounds. When they were alone, Mr. Heimerdinger informed his assistant that he had decided to take the third applicant.

"For God's sake, why?" exclaimed the assistant.

Mr. Heimerdinger sighed. "In the first place," he said, "she looked very intelligent to me. In the second place, it is none of your damn business. And in the third place, she's my wife's sister."

"Jiminy, Seth," screamed a hillbilly bride to her husband. "Yer beard is caught fire."

"I know it, I know it," he answered angrily. "Cain't you see me prayin' fer rain?"

That late lamented Army newspaper, the *Kiska Bear*, featured a story about a school teacher who said to her most precocious student (aged seven), "Tommy, if I lay one egg on the table and two on the chair, how many will I have altogether?" "Personally," answered Tommy, "I don't think you can do it."

Ben Huebsch, the publisher, wages a continuous and inexorable struggle with Louis Untermeyer for the punning championship of America that threatens to leave both contestants, not to mention their audience, in a state of utter coma. There was the day, for instance, when Ben announced, "I am going to sneeze." "At whom?" asked his partner, a long-suffering soul named Best. "At-choo," said Ben. And the time he disclosed, "My secretary is in love with fourteen soldiers, but she says it's platoonic." I think you'll agree that he really went too far, though, when he called a friend on the phone and said, "If buttercups are yellow, what color are hiccoughs?" "I give up," said the friend warily. "Burple," said Ben. They yanked out his phone a few minutes later.

I asked Untermeyer if he had any puns to match the above. "I most certainly have," he replied promptly, "and if you want to read them, you can just go out and buy my own anthology."

Getting back to Mr. Huebsch, he is, in addition to possessing a really rare sense of humor, one of the most tactful publishers in America. A pretty young authoress got a sample of his skill when he rejected a manuscript she had submitted. "Don't you think it any good at all?" she implored. Mr. Huebsch patted her paternally in the right place and assured her, "Good is hardly the word for it."

"Two hundred dollars for this beautiful sedan?" demanded an outraged motorist of a secondhand dealer. "Do you realize I've owned this car eight years and never had a wreck?" "What you mean," corrected the dealer, "is that you've owned this wreck eight years and never had a car."

"I'll never forget the morning we first reached Niagara Falls," confided Mrs. O'Connor. "My husband's face dropped about a mile." "You mean to say he was disappointed?" asked Mrs. Geis incredulously. "Not at all," Mrs. O'Connor assured her. "He fell over the rim."

Two buzzards were lazily winging over the Arizona desert when Howard Hughes' jet-propelled plane suddenly went hurtling by, its exhausts belching flame and smoke. The buzzards silently watched it disappear into the Western sky, and then one of them found his voice. "Holy carrion," he said. "Was that bird in a hurry!" "Listen, Lucius," opined the other, "you'd be in a hurry too if your tail was on fire."

You probably have met your share of refugees who felt for some strange reason that they had to tell you immediately what big shots they had been in Germany before that *Schwein* Hitler, etc., etc. It got so bad at one time that an insignificant little German dachshund turned up his nose at a couple of wire-haired terriers who tried to make friends. "Don't tink I alvays vus chust a dachshund," sniffed the foreigner. "Back home I vus a Saint Bernard!"

A spy at one of Mr. Toscanini's rehearsals at the National Broadcasting Company reports that the maestro shattered even his own record for breaking batons over his knee, tearing up sheet music, and raising hell in general when a harp player, required to play one single note in a symphony, plucked the wrong string. The orchestra began over again and when the time came for the harpist to play his note, he was so flustered that he repeated his mistake. The maestro strode from the rehearsal in speechless rage. When the orchestra assembled for the actual broadcast the next afternoon, the harpist discovered that every string but the one he would be called upon to pluck had been removed from the instrument.

Two poems cherished by Herbert Ellefson:

1. I sneezed a sneeze into the air,
   It fell to earth, I know not where.
   But hard and froze were the looks of those
   In whose vicinity I snoze.

2. 'Twas in a restaurant they met
   Brave Romeo and Juliet.
   He had no cash to pay his debt
   So Romeo'd what Juli'et.

Football Coach Bo McMillin once had a great back on his team whose conceit threatened to undo him. McMillin never overlooked a chance to take him down a peg. One day the back picked up a fumbled ball on his own three-yard line and galloped the length of the field for a game-winning touchdown.

In the locker room McMillin controlled his elation. "You started too slow," he told the back. "You went down the wrong side of the field; there were fewer men to take out on the left side. And I didn't like the way you stiff-armed their safety man. Seems to me it would have been better to side-step him."

The back looked serious for a minute, and then said, "There's only one other thing I'd like to know, Coach. How was it for distance?"

She was a lovely, warmhearted little thing, and she loved her "feller" devotedly. Her only fault was blind jealousy—particularly of her equally attractive roommate, Bertha.

One evening the boy's old college chum went to dinner with them, and brightened perceptibly at the suggestion that Bertha make a fourth to the party. The girl demurred. "I'm sick and tired of this idiotic jealousy," her lover declared. "Now you take this nickel and call Bertha, or everything is over between us."

Visibly cowed, she departed in the direction of the phone booth. Five minutes later she was back. "Bertha says she's sorry," was the report, "but she worked late at the office today, and she's so tired she's going straight to bed. . . . And here's your nickel back."

William Saroyan once set out to interview Marc Connelly, of *Green Pastures* fame. He reported later, "Connelly is one of the most interesting talkers I ever encountered. At the conclusion of the interview I was so hoarse I couldn't say another word for fifteen minutes."

An irate member accosted the secretary of a London literary club and said, "Give me your advice, John. I have been deliberately insulted by Colonel So-and-So. Without preamble he said to me, 'Sir, I will give you fifty pounds if you resign your membership in this club.' What do you think I ought to do about it?" "That's obvious," said the secretary tartly. "Hold out for a better offer."

If Dr. Morris Fishbein, medical editor of the *Encyclopaedia Britannica*, and Lord knows what else, can tell this story in print, it must be okay. The heroine is a lady who went to a very ritzy clinic for a thorough checkup. The first doctor said, "Let me see your tongue." The second said, "Let me feel your pulse." A dozen other specialists took their turn, and the lady became more and more disturbed. Finally, a little man turned up who was dressed in blue dungarees and carried a mop and slop bucket. "Good heavens," gasped the lady. "What are you going to do?" "Be calm, madam," he answered. "I'm just going to wash your transom."

Joseph Fliesler, of *Look* magazine, told me the story about the fellow who decided to sell a long-treasured letter signed by Thomas Jefferson. When the transaction was completed, the dealer remarked, "I'd have given you $50.00 more if it hadn't been for those stains. Looks like somebody used ink eradicator on part of this document"

"That was me," said the seller. "A fool named Button Gwinnett or something wrote 'See me about this' acrost the bottom, but I managed to get it all off."

When William Travers left his home town for the big city, everybody knew he would make good. The boy had everything; his only defect was a pronounced stutter. Some years later, when Travers had become a rich man on the Stock Exchange, a boyhood friend met him on Broad Street and greeted him joyfully. "W-w-w-well, well!" said Travers. "It's mighty f-f-fine to s-s-see a b-b-boyhood chum once m-m-more!" "Why, William," laughed his friend, "you're an even bigger stutterer than you were at home." "Y-y-yes," replied Travers. "Y-y-you see, this is a d-d-damn sight b-b-bigger city."

This one really *has* whiskers!

Mike to Pat: Bejabbers, and where did you get thim black eyes and bloody nose?

Pat to Mike: Shure, an' that Eyetalian Consolino picked a fight with me.

Mike to Pat: And you, a great big son o' the old sod let a peewee runt of an Eyetalian beat the likes of you?

Pat to Mike: You shouldn't go on that way, Mike. Never spake ill of the dead!

Travers was fond of parrots, and had several in his home. One day he spotted a beauty in a pet shop, but noticed that it didn't utter a sound. He summoned the proprietor and inquired, "C-c-can this b-b-bird t-t-talk?" The proprietor chuckled. "Mister," he said, "if that parrot couldn't talk better than you, I'd cut his blooming head off."

Greenstone had been in Miami for about a week when he felt the urge to do a little gambling. His friend explained that reformers had clamped the lid down tight on Dade County, but that one back room was running surreptitiously in an obscure night club. Just before they entered, the friend warned, "You realize, of course, that this place is crooked. The wheel is fixed, and I think the dice are loaded." "Not so loud," pleaded Greenstone. "They might hear us and not let us in."

Max Schulman, in his highly amusing *Barefoot Boy with Cheek*, speaks with awe of the hero's grandfather, who sued the Reynolds Tobacco Company for a million dollars. His contention was that he had smoked so many Camels that he got a hump on his back.

Tower Books has revived Ring Lardner's classic story of a bush-league ballplayer, *You Know Me, Al*, with Lardner's own hilarious preface. It begins, "An introduction to this book was written by Will Rogers, but the Scribner boys threw it out on the ground that it was better than the book. However, there was one remark of Mr. Rogers which I think should be preserved. Referring to me, he wrote, 'He is undoubtedly the biggest—.' The rest of the sentence is so blurred as to be indecipherable."

An English lord was taken to one of the first Army-Navy football games ever played. It was a bitter struggle, and a lot of players were hurt. "I say," commented the Englishman after a scrimmage that left two men prostrate on the field, "wouldn't it be simpler if they gave each team a ball?"

Mrs. Hibbs sought her hostess and inquired, "What's become of that pretty waitress who was passing the cocktails?" "I'm sorry," apologized the hostess. "Were you looking for a drink?" "Thank you, no," said Mrs. Hibbs. "I was looking for my husband."

If you are bothered by the memory of some embarrassing moment of your own, pause for a second to consider the plight of a recent city commissioner out West. Chosen honorary foreman of a widely ballyhooed rodeo, he made a spectacular first-night entry on a snow-white charger, circled the arena while the city's notables and cowboy performers applauded politely, and pulled up before a battery of microphones—where the horse promptly threw him on his face.

An old grad was belittling the quality of present-day gridiron warriors. "When I was in college," he told the coach, "I helped Williams trim Amherst three years in succession." "Zatso," nodded the coach. "Which team did you say you were playing for?"

Boyce House's tall tales of Texas have become legendary. The air is so bracing down there, he avers, that the State Chamber of Commerce had to hire an Easterner to shoot himself so they could start a cemetery. At the last minute he rued his bargain and ran for his life. Pistol Pete lassoed him, and declared when he brought him in, "This dude was runnin' so fast his vest pocket was dippin' up sand."

In a remote corner of the state, the first motorcycle Sam'l ever had seen chugged by. Sam'l seized his rifle and fired. "Git the varmint?" asked his wife. "Nope," said Sam'l. "I still hear the critter but I shore made it turn that man loose." A few weeks later, Sam'l enjoyed his first train ride, but got into a bit of a row with the news butcher. He bought a banana, and the next time the butcher came through the car he demanded his money back. "That thing you sold me," he claimed, "has got too much cob."

Pyote, Texas, is the only town in the U.S.A. that has a sign reading, "You are now entering our city," and is able to use the back of the same sign for "You are now leaving our city." Pyote's leading—in fact, its only lawyer—once was sued himself and cannily decided to handle his own case. "Gentlemen of the jury," he declaimed, "I know it is an old adage that the lawyer who conducts his own lawsuit hath a fool both for a client and an attorney." He had to rush off to Dallas while the jury was still out, but that night a friend wired him "Old adage unanimously upheld."

A Fort Worth newspaper printed a personal ad that read, "If John Blank, who deserted his wife and baby twenty-one years ago, will return, said baby will knock hell out of him." A cub reporter on the same sheet referred in his first story to a "local schoolteacher." The editor advised, "Son, always use the name of the city; never use the word 'local.'" The next day the youngster covered the operation on a tycoon and reported, "The surgeon used a Fort Worth anaesthetic."

Can you take a few more tales of tipplers? . . . One of them explained to a flabbergasted judge, "The whole thing is the fault of the bad company I got into. I had a whole bottle of Scotch and was with four muggs who don't touch a drop!" . . . Another explained a multitude of cuts and bruises, "I was carrying a drunk home—and he dropped me." . . . A third gravely informed an outraged dowager, "Madam, thish unforshunate ashident would not have occurred if you hadn't shtepped between me—hic—and the shpitoon!" . . . An awed bystander watched the great W. C. Fields in action, and asked, "Don't you ever get the D. T.'s?" "That's hard to say, my chickadee," responded Fields. "In these parts it's impossible to tell where Hollywood ends and the D. T.'s begin." . . . Ex-Police-Commissioner Valentine told a banquet audience, "I'll say one thing for habitual drunks: when they sober up, they keep both feet on the ground. They can't lift 'em!"

One of the snappiest beginnings to a story I remember was one dashed off by Stephen Leacock in a parody of Horatio Alger:

"How about a job?"

The man on the ladder, building a house, looked down at the manly little fellow who piped up with this question. Something in the lad's intelligent eyes and straightforward mien appealed to the man. He threw a brick at him.

They were burying Lenkowsky, a godless and unsavory character who had never been near a place of worship in his entire lifetime, and the services were necessarily conducted by a rabbi who had never heard of the man before. He noticed that the family seemed prosperous and thought he'd earn a higher fee if he poured on the encomiums indiscriminately. After ten minutes of raving over the unparalleled virtues of the late lamented as a father, husband, and boss, Mrs. Lenkowsky, whose expression had grown more and more baffled, finally nudged her son and whispered, "For God's sake, Boris, go up there and make sure it's papa!"

An army corporal hauled a man into a police station and charged him with lifting his wallet. "I'm guilty, Judge," confessed the man. "Please give me a sentence and a divorce, too." "Why a divorce?" asked the judge. "I opened the corporal's wallet," said the defendant, "and the only thing I found in it was three pictures of my wife."

At the Dutch Treat Club, John Golden declared that the following was probably the oldest theatrical story extant:

An old Shakespearean ham actor told the manager of the opry house in a one-horse burg he was playing that he didn't feel in the mood for *Hamlet*, and had decided to do *Othello* instead. "Not on your life," bellowed the manager. "I got a sign up in a barbershop window saying the bill was *Hamlet* tonight, and it's *Hamlet* you're going to play." "Okay," said the actor wearily, "but in that case you will have to advance me a dime to go over to that barbershop and get a shave." "Advance you a dime, eh?" mused the manager. "Oh, hell, play *Othello*."

"Let's see if we can locate the cause of your neurosis," said the psychoanalyst to the harassed soul before him. "What kind of work do you do?" "I sort oranges," was the reply. "I don't think I understand," the doctor admitted. "Please elaborate."

"All day," the patient explained, "oranges keep pouring down a chute. I stand at the bottom and sort them. Big oranges go into a crate on one side, little ones into a crate on the other, medium ones into a crate in the center. See?" "I do," said the psychoanalyst, "but certainly there's nothing in that to upset you. It sounds easy enough to me." "Easy!" cried the patient. "Don't you realize it means decisions! decisions! decisions!— all day long!"

Two young aviators had had a couple too many in the local tavern and got lost on their way back to the Orlando Air Base. Suddenly one of them stopped and said, "Hey, Tom, I think we've gotten into a cemetery. Here's a gravestone." "Whose is it?" asked Tom. The aviator lit a match, peered at the stone, and said, "I don't recognize his name, but he sure lived to a fine old age—225." "Wow," ejaculated his friend. "Who was it, Methuselah?" The aviator lit another match. "No," he reported. "It was some jerk who was named Miles to Miami."

Rastus's boss was inclined to overlook his tardiness, but one morning he lost his temper. "You're late again," he thundered. "Don't you use the alarm clock I gave you?" "Yassir, every night," said Rastus. "Well," said the boss. "Why don't you get up when the alarm goes off?" "Dat's de trouble, Mr. Johnson," said Rastus. "It always seems to go off while I'm asleep."

Leo Slezak, the German tenor, was once singing *Lohengrin* at the Metropolitan when an inept stagehand yanked the prop swan-boat off stage before he had a chance to enter it. Slezak, possessed of a robust sense of humor, and ready for any emergency, abruptly stopped singing and called loudly into the wings, "When does the next swan leave?"

Another time Slezak was singing in *Die Walküre*. The lady who was set to play the role of Sieglinde took sick at the last moment, and unbeknownst to Slezak, an understudy was rushed into the part. She came on stage behind him and warbled *"Ich bin Sieglinde"* ("I am Sieglinde"). Slezak wheeled about in surprise, clicked his heels, bowed, and said, "My name is Leo Slezak."

A hardy Indian medicine man was dangling his feet from a raft in Palm Beach, watching the great white fathers roughing it in their primitive cabanas. Suddenly a beautiful and voluptuous mermaid popped up from the sea and sat down beside him. The Indian looked her over for a moment and said, "How?"

Grady had been trying to make O'Leary pay off a poker debt for months. Cornered, O'Leary finally gave Grady a promissory note, and sighed with relief, "Thank God, that's paid!"

A young wife whose husband had been stationed on a lush South Sea isle for three years visited her doctor in a state of acute depression. "He's fallen head-over-heels for those native belles," she complained. "Every letter is filled with gushing descriptions of them. I can't bear much more of it. How can I get him over his mad infatuation?" "Well," said the doctor, "the Army long ago discovered a substance called saltpetre which has a very sobering effect when administered in a man's food. If we could only get some to your husband, he'd soon be himself again. Let's see. Can you make fudge?" "Oh, yes," said the wife. "I always made the best chocolate fudge in school—and Henry just loves it." "Good," said the doctor. "Send Henry a big box of fudge and put plenty of that saltpetre in it."

The wife took the doctor's suggestion. She didn't hear from her husband for seven full weeks. When a letter finally came, she tore it open with feverish hands. It began, "Dear Friend."

A small stockholder in a great corporation felt that he had been unjustly treated in a new stock issue, and registered his complaint with the head of the outfit. "You are absolutely right," admitted that gentleman, "but I beg you not to press the point. Thousands of other stockholders would make equal demands, and you'd upset the whole applecart." "You remind me of my older brother when we both were kids," said the complainant wryly. "Every night after we had been put to bed he'd start beating my brains out. The minute I started to bawl, he'd whisper, 'Ss-s-sh! You'll wake mama.'"

Joan Davis complained to a waitress that her tea looked pretty weak. "Lady," said the waitress, "you'd be weak too if you'd been dunked eighty-eight times in a cup of hot water."

A camouflage battalion was training in Louisiana, and Mike and Jamie were doing very nicely as the front and rear, respectively, of a gentle-eyed cow. Suddenly Jamie gave Mike a vigorous kick and muttered, "Run like hell." "What's the matter?" said Mike. "Matter?" echoed Jamie. "Here comes the general's wife with a milk pail."

A lovesick young accountant had regaled his room-mate for weeks with tales of the beauty, breeding, and brilliance of his latest conquest, Hyacinth. Finally he produced her for dinner. The roommate had already marked her down to bargain basement proportions in his own mind when the accountant unwittingly provided the clincher. "Want to know what I'm giving Hyacinth for a birthday present?" he asked (Hyacinth was sitting on his lap at the time). "I've bought her a wonderful T-R-A-V-E-L-L-I-N-G case." The roommate whispered, "S-s-sh! She can hear you." "She won't understand," said the lover confidently. "She spells 'traveling' with one 'L.'"

The late Sam Harris once bought a play because he heard that excellent actor, Arnold Daly, reading it aloud to a group and found himself profoundly moved by it. It turned out to be one of the most dismal flops of his career. "This has been a great lesson to me," he said. "That's what I get for letting a $2,000-a-week actor read a drama to me and getting a $100-a-week actor to play it."

A Yankee reporter asked a Negro preacher in a southern town what subjects he favored for his weekly sermons. "Ah gives 'em repertory," said the preacher. "Sometimes love, sometimes baptism, sometimes de joys of de hereafter." "Do you ever touch on anything like chicken stealing?" ribbed the reporter. "Definitely no," said the preacher. "Ah has discovered dat subjects of dat description throws what one might call a coldness over de meetin'."

One of New York's favorite columnists is Louis Sobol. Sobol is the man who discovered that a Ubangi is the only human on earth who can seal a letter with a kiss—after it's in the mailbox.

The young daughter of one of his newspaper pals came home from Sunday school with an illustrated card in her hand. "What have you got there, honey?"

asked the father. "Nothing much," said the little girl. "Just an ad about heaven."

A star reporter, when Louis was still an office boy in short pants, was assigned to cover the last days of the railroad magnate, W. H. Harriman. The press had quarters in an exclusive hotel in near-by Tuxedo. After the millionaire had passed away, the newsman turned in his expense account. It was a whopper. The managing editor studied it grimly, and commented, "If this is Mr. Harriman's will you're showing me, it's worth a story on its own."

Phil Silvers, bespactacled Hollywood comic, once had a crush on Olivia de Haviland, for which no reader, I'm sure, can blame him. She went out with him several times, but when he asked her to the Academy Award dinner, social highwater mark of the season, she said, "I'll go with you—but you must promise to leave off those glasses. They make you look so silly."

Silvers promised—and kept his word. He arrived at her door that evening in white tie and tails, with a corsage of orchids—and a seeing-eye dog.

"Miss Jones," said the science professor, "would you care to tell the class what happens when a body is immersed in water?" "Sure," said Miss Jones. "The telephone rings."

"I would like to reaffirm my belief in Buddha," said Hop Lee May, "but on the other hand, there is a great deal to be said for oleomargarine."

Shortly after Mike's funeral, the priest called on his widow Norah. "I've got the lazy good-for-nothing working at last." "What talk, Norah," said the priest, "and him dead a week." "True, Father," she agreed, "but I had him cremated and now I've got his ashes in an hourglass."

Chester Kerr knows a man who is the ninth child of a persevering couple who previously had produced eight straight girls in a row. When the happy sire heard that he had at last had a boy, he went on a week-long celebration that broke several records. On the seventh day, somebody asked him, "Whom does it look like; you or your wife?" "I don't know," the proud parent chortled happily. "We haven't looked at his face yet."

Plotkin suspected a catch when they offered him a room in the swanky Rockaway Ritzmore on the American plan for ten dollars a day. When he saw the size of the portions at his first dinner he was sure of it. As the waiter planked the meat course in front of him, Plotkin rose dramatically to his feet, pointed his knife at the morsel of meat, and announced loudly, "Waiter, at home, there's more than that on the plate when I'm finished."

"How I first met your mother is not a story for little ears like yours," a father told his son from behind the evening newspaper. "But one thing I can tell you. It certainly cured me of whistling."

Admiral Byrd was showing his trophies to an admiring visitor. "By rights," he said, "this silverware should have been given to my dogs. They discovered the pole first."

A giddy hostess once asked Professor Einstein to explain his theory of relativity in "a few well-chosen words."

"I will tell you a story instead," said the scientist. "I once was walking with a blind man, and remarked that I would like a glass of milk.

" 'What is milk?' asked my blind friend.

" 'A white liquid,' I replied.

" 'Liquid I know. But what is white?'

" 'The color of a swan's feathers.'

" 'Feathers I know. What is a swan?'

" 'A bird with a crooked neck.'

" 'Neck I know. But what is crooked?'

"Thereupon I lost patience. I seized his arm and

straightened it. 'That's straight,' I said, and then I bent it at the elbow. 'That's crooked.'

" 'Ah,' said the blind man, 'now I know what you mean by milk.'

"Do you still want to know about relativity?" The hostess decided to change the subject.

During the last boom, the members of the Tannenbaum Country Club decided to show the world how fashionable they had become by staging a fox hunt. Every member, it was agreed, would supply one hunting dog, and the steward was dispatched to locate a fox. On the morning of the great event, the self-conscious members gathered in resplendent red jackets, and set off for the chase, while the president and vice-president posted themselves on the clubhouse verandah to follow the action through binoculars. What nobody knew was that Member Finkowitz had unwittingly contributed a bitch in heat. When the chase had been in progress for a half hour the vice-president asked anxiously, "Nu? How is it going?" The president put down the binoculars and said, "I can't understand it. The fox is running fifth."

Will Morrisey, reminiscing about the early days of radio, when you had to clamp a set of earphones on your head to catch a program, swears that one "artist" declared, "My next number is a special request from the Mikado." A short time later he announced, "I just received another telegram. It reads, 'You're coming in great, Joe. (Signed) The Mikado' "

"Don't think that you can get away with anything, just because I'm inexperienced," complained a young bride. "That flour you sold yesterday is too tough." The grocer, who thought he had heard everything, threw up his hands. "Don't deny it," continued the bride. "I made biscuits with that flour, and my husband broke two teeth trying to bite one."

"This year," the announcer at the Atlantic City beauty contest told a breathless world, "we are going to judge the entries on their intelligence as well as their physical attributes." The mental quiz began with a problem from James (Harry, not William): "Why can't a locomotive sit down?" Poor Miss Altoona couldn't answer. "Because it has a tender behind," explained the questioning wizard. Miss Altoona got a zero. Now will you go to college?

"I'm looking for the spaghetti factory," a stranger in a shiny new Buick told two old characters lounging in front of the post office. "Never heard tell of no spaghetti factory around here," said one of them. "I wouldn't have the faintest idea where it is." After the stranger had driven off, the other native said, "Do you suppose that fellow could have meant the macaroni factory?" "I'll bet you're right," said Zeb to the first one. "Let's catch him."

They hollered at the top of their lungs and the stranger waited for them to overtake him. "Could it have been the macaroni factory you were looking for?" said Zeb. "I guess you're right," acknowledged the stranger. "Where is the macaroni factory?" "Oh," said Zeb. "We don't know where that is either."

A regular army unit adopted as mascot an amiable bulldog who was named "Sergeant" and had three stripes duly sewn on his blanket. One day the pooch chewed up a stack of vital documents. "Why didn't you stop him?" roared the officer in charge. "I didn't dare," the clerk answered. "He outranks me."

Herman Peterson, author of *Country Chronicle*, moved his family to an upstate farm because he thought the tranquil surroundings would help him in his writing. Neighbors grew suspicious when he made no efforts to cultivate his acres, and the nosiest of them came over to investigate. Peterson admitted that he was interested in neither cows, chickens, nor cash crops. "What are you goin' to raise then?" persisted the farmer. "Children," said Peterson desperately. "Shucks," commented the farmer. "Around here, we consider that a side line."

A story from the Dexter Fellows archives concerns a lion trainer who advertised for an assistant. A young Negro applicant appeared who stated confidently, "I'se your man, boss. The lion don't live what can scare me." "Good," said the trainer. "We need a man to stick his head in the lion's mouth. It's really very simple. Think you can do it?" "Only thing bothers me," said the applicant, "is what happens if dat lion suddenly decides to close his mouf?" "In that case," the trainer assured him solemnly, "you can take the rest of the day off."

There's probably not a word of truth in this story, but it concerns a time when George, later George V, was a little boy at school. Temporarily out of funds, he wrote a heartbreaking letter to his august grandmother, the good Queen Victoria, begging pecuniary assistance. The good queen didn't fall for it. Instead, she wrote him a sharp note telling what happened to little boys who exceeded their allowances. Back came a letter which read, "My dear Grandmamma: I am sure you will be glad to know that I need trouble you no longer for money. I sold your last letter to one of the tutors for three pounds."

"I wonder," said the Sunday-school teacher, "what little boy or girl can tell me the name of that wonderful place with enormous marble pillars, and golden angels, and divine music, and perfumed air, where all of us go if we are good?" "Shucks," said the class in chorus. "Everybody knows that. Radio City Music Hall!"

Henry Klee in Toronto sends the story of the captain of a freighter who took on two new hands, one a Kirkcaldy man without a letter of recommendation, the other a man from Dundee possessed of abundant documentary evidence as to his honesty. They had not been long at sea when they encountered rough weather, and the Dundee man, crossing the deck with a bucket in his hand, was swept overboard. The Kirkcaldy man saw what had happened and leisurely sought out the captain.

"Dae ye mind yon man frae Dundee," he said, "that ye engaged, wi' the fine character?"

"Yes," said the captain. "What of it?"

"He's awa' wi' yer bucket."

Dr. Saunders gave his eighty-year-old patient a curious stare. "I've been practicing for two decades," he stated, "and I'm darned if anybody has ever come to me before with a complaint like yours. What do you mean: 'your virility's too high'?" The old man sighed gently. "It's all up in my head," he explained.

A timid, mousey little man tapped on the arm of the formidable gent who had been sitting next to him at theatre. "I don't suppose you chance to be Hector Periwinkle of Hartsdale, New York?" he hazarded. "No, I don't," said the f.g. "What's it to you?" "Just this, sir," squeaked Mousey. "I am—and that's his umbrella you're taking."

Gypsy Rose Lee tells the story of a chorus girl in her company who grumbled, "Why ain't I never invited to swell parties like you are, Gypsy?" "It's because your conversation is too limited," Gypsy told her. "Those fashionable people are mighty smart. Everyone talks like an expert on 'Information Please.' Why don't you read a book and broaden your horizons?"

The chorus girl thought that was an excellent idea. She read a book. A short time later Gypsy took her along to a publishers' party. She said nothing for the first half-hour and then suddenly startled the assemblage by inquiring in a loud voice, "Wasn't that too bad about Marie Antoinette?"

The girl with the big blue eyes said, "I'm troubled by a nasty little wart that I'd like to have removed." "You've made a slight error," said the man in the white coat. "I'm a doctor. The divorce lawyer is three doors down the hall."

Just about the dreariest jokes in the world are the inevitable accounts of drunken husbands trying to sneak into bed without arousing their terrible-tempered wives. One of the better ones, however, concerns the wily party who paused en route in the kitchen and laboriously tied all the pots, pans, and trays he could find to a rope. He then proceeded upstairs, dragging the rope behind him, and muttering happily, "She'll never hear me in all this racket."

Huey Long, smartest and most dangerous of American demagogues, constantly kept a finger on the public pulse. A henchman reported one day, "A lot of your constituents don't see eye to eye with you on that traction bill, Boss." "Stay right on the ball, Jim," advised Long. "If ever enough of them oppose it to become a majority, I'll come out against it myself."

Somebody once asked Long, "Do you think we'll ever have Fascism in America, Huey?" "Sure," said the wily Long. "Only here we'll call it anti-Fascism."

Young Connelly, whose father had been hanged as a horse-thief, experienced a little trouble in filling out an application blank for life insurance. The cause of his mother's death was easy: double pneumonia. It took several minutes, however, before he found the proper words to explain the old man's demise: "My father was taking part in a heavily attended public function when the platform gave way."

Walter Pater was once invited to admire a hideous and ornate wedding present, bestowed upon his niece. The great aesthete shuddered slightly, and remarked, "Very handsome. Very decorative. Very expensive, I'm sure. But for God's sake, *don't let them make any more of them!*"

Mr. Burrell liked the apartment well enough, but was bothered by some small stains on the ceiling of the study. "Don't worry about them," said the renting agent. "The last man who occupied this apartment was a professor who always was experimenting with some funny smelling chemical."

"I see," said Burrell. "Then those spots must be the chemical."

"Not at all," said the renting agent. "They're the professor."

*

One of the looniest—and funniest—acts in the big time today is that of "Professor Lamberti," an artist who plays the xylophone so vociferously that most of his clothes fly off in the process. The eminent Prof. parks a huge wad of chewing gum under his instrument before he begins, leers at his audience, and announces that his first number will be "The Stiffening Movement from Rigor Mortis." He adds "You've heard xylophonists of every rank, but I'll bet you never heard one as rank as me." The Prof. is called upon for encore after encore. The fact that a beautiful assistant is doing a provocative strip tease behind him may have something to do with the spectators' insatiable appetite for the xylophonic interpretation of "If Wishing Could Make It So." Prof. Lamberti avers that one music-lover was so carried away by the performance, it cost him fourteen bucks to get back to the theatre.

*

A farmer, looking mighty uncomfortable in his Sunday best, stamped up to the ticket agent at a tiny wayside station on the Erie, and thundered, "Why in tarnation don't you fellers get that Sunday local travelin' on time?" "What's it to you, Seth?" inquired the agent, placidly chewing on a toothpick. "You ain't never rode on that train in your life." "'Tain't that," mourned Seth. "But our fool preacher times his sermons to end when that local whistles fer the Main Street crossing, and it's been a full forty minutes late now three Sundays running!"

*

The house surgeon of a London hospital was attending to the injuries of a woman whose arm had been severely bitten. As he was dressing the wound, he frowned, and remarked, "I can't imagine what sort of creature must have bitten you. This is too small for a horse's bite, and too large for a dog's." "Oh, sir," explained the patient, "it wasn't an animal at all; it was another lydy!"

Book publishers' publicity departments often send out the silliest and most insipid material about their authors—routine drivel that editors hurl into the trash basket without a second thought. Occasionally, however, one hard-pressed publicist has a real inspiration. Rinehart & Company, for instance, certainly did right by their volcanic author, Philip Wylie, when they distributed a monograph about him by Maggie Harriman, so clever and quotable that a hundred newspapers printed excerpts from it. "Bad writers," she concluded, "usually can't wait to express themselves, but for most of the good ones, like Wylie, the act of composition is a form of torture, rigidly self-imposed. One awestruck colleague remarked, 'When Phil comes to grips with literature, boy, he don't fool with it.' He is a born crusader, viewing his own violence with a certain humorous detachment. 'You are God's Angry Man,' a friend told him. 'Oh, I don't know,' said Wylie. 'Maybe I'm God's Little Acher.'"

Legendary is the story of the cloak-and-suiter who came home lamenting the loss of a crisp new ten-dollar bill. "I looked in de west pockets, de two pants pockets, and de right pocket of mine overcoat, and it ain't there!' "How about de left pocket of de overcoat?" suggested his wife. "I couldn't look dere," said the unhappy man. "Dot's de lest pocket I got. If it wasn't in dere, I'd drop dead!"

The newspapers reported a wild fracas at a party in Staten Island recently that ended with one swain bopping his fiancée on the head with a meat chopper. In court he wiped away a tear and exclaimed, "She was the most loving and affectionate girl that ever walked God's earth." One reporter headed his story "Fête Worse Than Death"; he was pretty sore when they blue-pencilled it.

A Hollywood reporter asked Gene Kelly, "When did you first begin to like girls?" Kelly's forthright answer was, "The minute I discovered they weren't boys."

A street hawker set up his telescope on Fifty-seventh Street, opposite the Ritz Tower, and was doing such a land-office business at ten cents a look that Officer Flannigan strolled over to investigate. The placard on the telescope read, "One dime to see the full moon, Venus, Mars, Jupiter, and Greta Garbo's private suite on the seventeenth floor!"

"Do you know anything of my wife's whereabouts?" Mr. Ketcham asked his cook. "Yes, sir," was the prompt answer. "She put them in the wash."

Russell B. Hopkins is preoccupied with stories about cross-eyed citizens. His local board of education, he tells me, discharged a cross-eyed teacher because they couldn't see eye to eye with her and she couldn't control her pupils. He had another friend who was so cross-eyed that when he cried the tears ran down his back. They finally took him to the hospital, suffering from bacteria. As for Ben Turpin, the world's most famous cross-eyed comedian, Mr. Hopkins declares he last was heard of in Miami, Florida, looking for the Northwest Mounted Police.

The height of specialization, initiated provincials may tell you, has been achieved by American Industry, but I defy you to find anything to compare with this ex-cerpt from an "Admiralty Stores List," printed in London's dignified New Statesman and Nation:

POTS, Chamber, plain.
POTS, Chamber, with Admiralty monogram in blue, for hospital use.

POTS, Chamber, fluted, with royal cipher in gold, for
    Flag Officers only.

POTS, Chamber, round, rubber, for lunatics.

The list goes on and on, but by this time, perhaps,
you have the general idea.

The lure of wartime wages in a munitions plant
brought Sambo north to Massachusetts for the first
time. He didn't take to the winter weather at all.
"Boy, will I be glad to get away from this ice and snow,
and back to St. Augustine again," he declared vehemently. The foreman sympathized, "I guess you have
to be born and raised in this climate to stand it properly." Sambo regarded the foreman incredulously, and
said, "You don't mean to tell me, Boss, that folks live
here when there ain't no war?"

The story of Cadet François and Lisette, the most
beautiful courtesan in France, is one of the best-known
in the world. It is not only a stand-by of anthologists,
but has been turned into a "black-out" sketch in musical
revues, and expanded by Alexander Woollcott, as was
his amiable fashion, into a story padded enough to earn
him a fat fee from a national magazine.

Lisette, according to the legend, was in such universal
demand and had so much to offer, that the price for one
evening of her company soared to five thousand francs.
By coincidence, there were exactly five thousand students at St. Pierre Military College, and an ingenious
first-year man proposed a lottery: each cadet would chip
in one franc, and the winner with the five thousand
francs would date up the incomparable Lisette.

François was the lucky fellow—and did he enjoy himself! Lisette was both touched by his gratitude and en-

chanted by his ardor. "Tell me," she said with a languor-
ous sigh, "where did a stripling like you get five thousand francs for this rendezvous?" François explained
about the lottery. Lisette was deeply moved. "This is
the most touching tribute," she exclaimed, "that I have
ever been paid. And François, you have delighted me so
that I feel I must reward you further." She reached into
her stocking and produced a single franc. "Here, François," she said, "here is your stake back."

The English teacher took a piece of chalk and wrote
on the blackboard, "I didn't have no fun over the week
end." "Now, James," she commanded, "how should I
correct that?" "Get yourself a feller," suggested James.

A bachelor skunk visited a newly married pair of
skunks and was surprised to find an extra bed in their
room. When questioned, they explained, "We are expecting a little stinker in the spring."

The U. S. Marines' publication, Leatherneck, defines
a pedestrian as "a man who has two cars, a wife, and a
son in high school"; mal de mer as a Frenchman's way
of saying "You can't take it with you."

"What's your candid opinion of my new novel?"
asked an author anxiously. "It's worthless," was the
blunt reply. "I know," persisted the author, "but I'd
like it anyhow."

A girl in the booth of the Roxy Theatre demurred at selling a ticket to a youngster in the early afternoon. "Why aren't you in school?" she asked sharply. "It's okay, lady," he assured her. "I've got the measles."

Jackie Miles once played an engagement in a kosher summer camp. "The people couldn't have been nicer," he reported, "but I had to quit in the middle of the week. I got snow-blinded by all the sour cream."

The first time Nussbaum and Shapiro went to Shanghai, a pixie guide steered them into an opium den, and persuaded them to take a few puffs. "It had no effect on me whatever," boasted Nussbaum. "Me neither,"

echoed Shapiro. A few minutes later Nussbaum beat his breast soundly and declared, "My mind is made up. I'm buying control of General Motors." "Sorry," said Shapiro, "but I won't sell."

Wesleyan '49 reported ecstatically to Wesleyan '50, "Boy, it's happened to me! I'm in love. Prettiest girl in Smith. One of twins!" "Twins, huh?" said his younger friend. "How d'ya tell 'em apart?" "Nobody could ever fool me on my Angelina," boasted the Lothario. "Besides, her twin is stroke on the Yale crew."

David Ewen tells about the composer who signed to do the complete score for a musical comedy in ten days. "That will take a lot out of you," commented a well-wisher. "Not out of me," countered the composer, "but out of Tchaikowsky, Brahms, and Bach."

The day after Clancy hit New York from County Cork, his brother took him over to see the Central Park Zoo. "Was ye after likin' the menagerie?" asked his sister-in-law, when he got back to the flat. "The menagerie was wonderful and delightful," said Clancy, "but I couldn't stand the animals."

The Pinsky Brothers, burlesque entrepreneurs, noted with alarm that their most famous strip-teaser's once cuddlesome curves were swelling into behemothian bulges. "Maybe," suggested one, "we should make Trixie go on a diet." "It's too late for diets," said his brother glumly. "What we gotta do is make Trixie stop eating altogether!"

The G. & C. Merriam Company, which publishes the authentic Webster dictionaries, regrets that it cannot quite bring itself to print the following definition of a "boy" in its regular editions, but I think it will give as deep satisfaction to every reader of this book as it did to the editor. The authorship, unfortunately, is unknown; Merriam considers it "authentic folklore."

BOY: After a male baby has grown out of long clothes and triangles and has acquired pants, freckles, and so much dirt that relatives do not dare to kiss it between meals, it becomes a BOY. A boy is Nature's answer to that false belief that there is no such thing as perpetual motion. A boy can swim like a fish, run like a deer, climb like a squirrel, balk like a mule, bellow like a bull, eat like a pig, or act like a jackass, according to climatic conditions. He is a piece of skin stretched over an appetite. A noise covered with smudges. He is called a tornado because he comes at the most unexpected times, hits the most unexpected places, and leaves everything a wreck behind him. He is a growing animal of superlative promise, to be fed, watered, and kept warm, a joy forever, a periodic nuisance, the problem of our times, the hope of a nation. Every boy born is evidence that God is not yet discouraged of man. Boys faithfully imitate their dads in spite of all efforts to teach them good manners. A boy, if not washed too often and if kept in a cool, quiet place after each accident, will survive broken bones, hornets, swimming holes, fights, and nine helpings of pie.

STOP!
DON'T READ
TOO MANY
JOKES AT ONE TIME.
THEY'RE FUNNIER IN SMALL DOSES

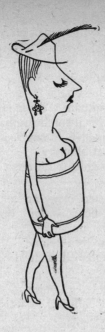

A FEW YOU-KNOW-WHATS

1. THERE was a young damsel named Carol
   Who liked to play stud for apparel.
   Her opponent's straight flush
   Brought a maidenly blush
   And a hasty trip home in a barrel.

2. There was a young man from Australia
   Who painted himself like a dahlia.
   The colors were bright,
   And the size was just right
   But the smell was a definite fahlia.

3. A magician who came from Vt.
   Sawed a woman in half for a stt.
   When she mildly asked whether
   He would put her together
   He replied "I've decided I wt."

4. A lovely young girl named Anne Heuser
   Declared that no man could surprise'er.
   But a fellow named Gibbons
   Untied her Blue Ribbons
   And now she is sadder Budweiser.

5. A lass who weighed many an oz.
   Used words that nice girls don't pronoz.
   When a prankster unkind
   Yanked her chair from behind
   Just to see, he explained, if she'd boz.

6. A lady from near Lake Louise
   Declared she was bothered by fleas.
   She used gasoline
   And later was seen
   Sailing over the hills and the trees.

7. There was an old monk in Siberia
   Whose existence grew steadily drearier
   Till he broke from his cell
   With a hell of a yell
   And eloped with the Mother Superior.

8. A merchant addressing a debtor
   Set down in the course of his lebtor
   "I choose to suppose
   A man knose what he ose
   And the sooner he pays it the bedtor."

9.　There was a young man in Devizes
　　Whose ears were of two different sizes.
　　The one that was small
　　Was of no use at all,
　　But the other won numerous prizes.

10.　A fellow named Crosby (not Bing)
　　Was asked by a hostess to sing.
　　He replied, "It is odd,
　　But I always mix 'God
　　Save the Weasel' and 'Pop Goes the King.'"

11.　A daring young fellow in Bangor
　　Sneaked a B-29 from its hangor.
　　When he crashed in the bay
　　Neighbors laid him away
　　In rather more sorrow than angor.

12. A lusty young wench in Toledo
    Had a very inflated libido.
    When a couple of Finns
    Made her mother of twins
    She just hollered with joy, "Oh, you keedo."

13. A senior at lunch in Purdue
    Discovered a mouse in his stew.
    Said the waiter, "Don't shout
    And display it about
    Or the profs will be wanting one too."

14. A daring young maid from Dubuque
    Risked a rather decided rebuque
    By receiving a prude
    In the absolute nude
    But he gasped, "If you only could cuque!"

15. A man stopped his girl friend in Brussels
    And charged, "You are wearing two bustles!"
    She declared, "That's not true;
    It's a thing I don't do.
    You are merely observing my muscles."

16. A gent who was definitely weird
    Declared, "This is just what I feared.
    Please pass me the Lux
    For a lot of wild ducks
    Have established a nest in my beard."

"Young man," said an irate father from the head of the stairs, "didn't I hear the clock strike four when you brought my daughter home?" "You did," admitted the daughter's escort. "It was going to strike eleven, but I grabbed it and held the gong so it wouldn't disturb your slumber." The father could only mutter, "Dawgone! Why didn't I think of that one in my courting days!"

A reverse twist of this story concerns the gay young mother who came home at three, and was dismayed to find her ten-year-old daughter waiting up in the library. "Darling," she cried, "I told you you didn't have to wait up for me." "I know," said the little one grimly, "but who's going to let Grandma in?"

The picture star stopped off at a Wilshire Boulevard specialty shop and announced, "I'd like a pair of shorts to wear around my gymnasium." "Excellent," said the bemused clerk, reaching behind him. "Don't you think we better measure it for size?"

This is a true story that was reported recently by the New York Sun.

A man named Rabinowitz came out of a restaurant just as a taxi was driving off. He yelled, "Taxi," and the driver stopped for him. "Bathgate and Tremont Avenues," he ordered. When the cab arrived there, Rabinowitz alighted, walked into Bronx police headquarters, emerged with two cops, and arrested the driver. It was Rabinowitz's taxicab.

A Kentucky colonel read aloud a recipe for roast ham. "Place the ham in a pot," it directed. "Soak it one day in bourbon and cook it for a while. The second day, add a bottle of Jamaica rum, and cook it for a while. The third day, add a bottle of port wine, and the fourth day some fine rye whiskey."

"How does that sound to you?" the colonel asked his old Negro cook. "I dunno about the ham," was the reply, "but it sure sounds like the makin's of mighty powerful gravy."

A peddler, his cart loaded with boxes of cheap stationery, advertised his wares in a loud voice at a Delancey Street corner, but attracted nary a customer. Nobody seemed to want a "box of genuine linen station'ry an' fifty envelopes for twenty-five cents." Suddenly, however, another hawker wheeled a bigger cart right next to the first one, and began bellowing, "Here y'are folks! Box of fine stationery an' fifty envelopes fer ten cents—one dime! Don't pay more!" The two men glared at each other. A crowd gathered first to watch, and then to buy out the stock of the ten-cent merchant completely. The *Tribune* reporter who caught the story declares that all Delancey Street bought enough stationery to satisfy five years' demand. Then everybody hung around to jeer at the disconsolate peddler who had thought he could get a quarter for his wares.

On a sudden hunch, the reporter followed the quarter-man when he wheeled his cart away. Two blocks down, he caught up with the ten-cent peddler. The two men shook hands gleefully and started dividing up the quarter-man's inventory. "It worked like a charm," chuckled the latter. "Let's try Mott Street next!"

On the Fitch Bandwagon radio program appeared a character named Horace who admitted he was so emaciated and run down that he didn't dare don a tuxedo for fear some nearsighted undertaker would bury him.

"You ought to start eating carrots," suggested a well-wisher. "I had a friend who was in even worse shape than you. His doctor prescribed a carrot diet—nothing but carrots morning, noon, and night. He stuck to it for a year."

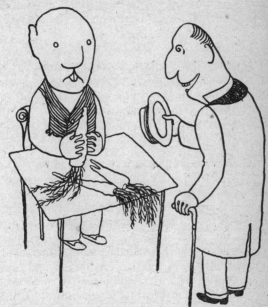

"Did the diet cure him?" asked Horace.

"I'm not sure," was the answer. "Every time I ask him how he feels, he just looks at me with his little pink eyes, and twitches his nose."

In the chorus girls' dressing room, Maizie boasted "Last night I coulda married a swell guy with $50,000." "Why didn't you?" asked Daisy. "Aw," said Maizie, "where was I gonna find $50,000?"

Somebody once asked Dr. Samuel Johnson why he hated the Scotch. "I do not hate them, Sir," insisted Dr. Johnson. "Neither do I hate frogs. But I'm damned if I like to have them hopping about my chambers."

"I looked too thin in my last picture," said a petulant film star to her camera man. "Can't you do something to make me look round?" The camera man did something and the star slapped him in the face.

One of those radio quacks who play God for a couple of thousand dollars a week to poor saps in distress received this letter from a worried admirer:

"I have been a soldier in the Pacific. My mother has epilepsy, and my father's nose and ears have fallen off, so you see they can't work. My two sisters are the sole support of the family. They are fast girls in Birmingham. My only brother is in the pen for murder and rape. I have two cousins who are Republicans. I am from the South and now that I'm out of uniform I naturally want to go back home to live.

"Mr. X., my problem is this: I am in love with a strip-tease artist in a town near ours and I want to ask her to be my wife. Dare I tell her about my two no-good Republican cousins?"

A Missouri school teacher offered a prize for the best "short short action story." Winner was a Negro lad with a bent for poetry:

"A mule in the barnyard—lazy and slick;
A boy with a pin on the end of a stick.
Boy slips behind him as still as a mouse:
Crêpe on the door of the little boy's house."

"It's wonderful, the power I got over dumb animals," Goldfarb confided to his friend. "Dogs, cats, horses, no matter how wild, they all come up and lick my hand."

"Hmph," sniffed the unimpressed friend. "Maybe if you'd eat with a knife and fork once in a while, they wouldn't be so friendly."

Indomitable perseverance has enabled Buck Crouse to complete a story that involves the appearance of the film star, Gloria de Haven, in a drama scheduled for Broadway unveiling on a Sunday evening. While the star is en route to the theatre, however, the subway system breaks down stranding her three miles north of Times Square and necessitating a postponement of the première to the following evening.

The name of this poignant tale, of course, is, "Sick Transit Gloria Monday."

When Ronny Anville won his fourth straight breach of promise suit he told reporters jubilantly, "These cases never bother me. No dame has been able to pin anything on me since I was ten months old!"

G. K. Chesterton once remarked, "The thing I hate most about an argument is that it always interrupts a discussion." Chesterton is also credited with the story of the wily bandit who finally was caught by the king's troopers. The king, who was fond of games and riddles, told the bandit, "You may make a statement. If you tell the truth in it, you will be shot. If you lie, you will be hanged." The bandit, without hesitation put everything in a fine mess by declaring, "Sire, I am going to be hanged."

There was an earthquake in Hollywood in the middle of the night a few years ago and one director had a harrowing experience. He dressed so hurriedly in the dark that when he got out into the middle of Sunset Boulevard he discovered that his jacket and pants matched.

Not too long ago Yale had a dean whose oldest son had a penchant for patronizing New Haven bars a bit too freely. One evening the old gentleman got word that the boy was really on the rampage and, eager to get him back into the sanctity of the home before the family name was irretrievably ruined, he dashed down Church Street to find him. He was charging along under full steam, distracted and angry, when a lady of the evening popped out of a doorway and accosted him. "Hi, pop," she caroled pleasantly. "Are you looking for a naughty little girl?" Unthinkingly the dean replied, "No, I'm looking for a naughty little boy." The girl recoiled in horror and exclaimed, "You nasty old man!"

When Sir John Ross was Lord High Chancellor of Ireland, he attended an art exhibition in his official capacity. The prize exhibit was a huge canvas entitled "The Dance of Salome." The Chancellor overheard two of Belfast's female art connoisseurs discussing its merits.

"What in the divil is this thing supposed to be, Maria?" demanded the first.

Maria consulted her catalogue, and answered, "It says here it's Solomon dancing for Herod."

"He niver done it, Maria," announced the first one firmly.

"Sure and he must have," said Maria tartly. "Else he couldn'ta been photaygraphed!"

A landlady assured a new boarder that his room contained a genuine feather bed. At two in the morning he limped to her door and hollered, "Madam, you'd better come upstairs and help me look for the feather."

The prize alibi of a batter who had stood at the plate in a pinch and watched three perfect strikes sail by was, "My bat didn't have no wood in it."

Three old cronies occupied their usual seats at the club where they could watch the pretty girls ankle by. Two of them at least had an added sparkle in their eyes, the reason for which was soon forthcoming. Spoke the first, "Well, gentlemen, I'm seventy-eight years old —durn near seventy-nine, in fact, and last month my wife presented me with a baby daughter." "Not bad," chuckled the second, "but not good either. I'll be eighty-four this March, and on Tuesday a son was born to my little bride. Weighs nine pounds, and he's handsome as his mother."

The third old gentleman was silent for a moment. Then he sighed, and said, "My friends, let me tell you a story. I'm eighty-eight. Used to hunt a lot, but I'm too old for that nonsense now. Last week I was strolling in the park and a cottontail came bounding out of the bushes. True to an old instinct, I raised my cane to shooting position, cried 'bang! bang!'—and the rabbit rolled over dead! A few minutes later I spied another cottontail. Again I simulated a rifle with my cane, and cried 'bang!' Again the rabbit dropped dead! What necromancy, what strange spell is this, I thought. Then, gentlemen, I glanced behind me. Ten paces to the rear was a young boy shooting with a real rifle!"

Rastus Green insisted on riding the merry-go-round at Coney Island before he ate his picnic lunch. His wife watched from the street with concentrated disapproval. When he came out, she remarked caustically, "Well, Rastus, yo' is spent yo' money, but whar is yo' been?"

George Jessel has a grievance against the Hotel Ambassador in Chicago, which he confided to Ashton Stevens. He was doing six shows a day at the Chicago Theatre, and tumbled into his bed at the Ambassador after the opening day, completely exhausted. Just as he was falling asleep, the revolving beacon from the Palmolive Building landed on his bed. Half awake, Jessel jumped to the floor, bowed, and sang two more songs.

The planners of a revival of an all-conquering musical comedy hit, says Oscar Hammerstein 2nd, must not only match the splendor of the original production, but the enhanced glamour of memory as well. He found that out when he revived *Show Boat* twenty years after Edna Ferber, Jerome Kern, and he first handed the script to Flo Ziegfeld. Old-timers shook their heads and said, "You'll never get scenery like the Old Master's," or "How can you hope to find anybody half as good as Charlie Winninger, Helen Morgan, and Edna May Oliver?"

This reminded Oscar of the time Diaghileff revived the ballet *Scheherazade*. A friend demanded, "Are you using the original Bakst designs?" "Yes," he answered, "but in much brighter colors." "Why?" asked the friend. "Because," said Diaghileff, "that's the way people remember them."

A farmer boy stuck his head into the kitchen of a neighbor and asked, "Kin you help me right a load of manure? It turned over in front of yer corn field." "Well, John," said the neighbor. "I reckon I'll eat my dinner first. Come and have some victuals with us." "I don't think Paw would like that," said the boy—but allowed himself to be persuaded. An hour later, the kindly neighbor said, "Let's listen to that Bob Hope radio program afore we tackle the truck." "I don't think Paw would like that," the boy said again—but he sat down and listened.

Finally, fully three hours after the boy's initial appearance, the neighbor rose, yawned, and said, "Now, John, let's right that manure truck of yours. Why don't we call your Paw to help us?"

"Oh, didn't I tell you?" said the boy. "Paw's under the manure."

An ex-corporal opened a machine shop in Brooklyn. "I've got the perfect name for it," he exulted. "The Diesel and Dosel Engine Works."

A librarian in Washington was stumped when a diffident young man asked for a book written by that eminent French author, Risqué.

When Colonel Putnam was alive, an old beggar accosted him, declaring that he was a veteran soldier. "You don't look it," said the Colonel bluntly, and barked, "Attention! Eyes right! Eyes front! Now, what comes next?" "Present alms," was the instant rejoinder. It won a handout.

At a recent session of the Thanatopsis Poker Club, a distinguished producer misplayed a hand, threw his cards angrily onto the table, and declared, "I am my own worst enemy." "Not while I'm in the room," F. P. Adams reminded him grimly.

Dr. Morris Fishbein was a member of the preview audience that was thrilled by *The Lost Weekend*. On the way out, he said it reminded him of the story of a saloonkeeper who had just unlocked his premises for the day's business when a pink elephant and a purple rhinoceros mooched up to the bar. "I'm sorry, boys," said the bartender. "He hasn't come in yet."

When the case of Finkelstein vs. Margolies was called, it developed that Finkelstein wanted back $300 he claimed he had loaned Margolies. Furthermore, he had two witnesses who swore they saw him give Margolies the money. Undaunted, Margolies jumped to his feet and yelled "Your honor, for every crooked witness Finkelstein produces who saw him give me the money, I will produce three what saw me give it back two days later." "Judge," Finkelstein yelled even louder, "just to show you what a liar Margolies is—*I never lent him the money in the first place!*"

The baggage car of the Georgia Central's slowest train contained two sacks of mail, a battered trunk, seven packages—and one live mule, with a destination tag tied around his neck. Just before the train reached Athens, the mule chewed up the tag. Mose, the brakeman, discovered the loss, and exclaimed, "Now what is we gonna do wid dis crazy mule? He done et up where he's goin'."

In Hollywood Sid Skolsky uncovered a writer who has perfected an invaluable system for approaching beautiful girls. He says, "I'm a stranger in town. Can you direct me to your house?"

In Chicago (unless the AP is kidding) Ignatz Zabrini wrapped a lead pipe around the head of a man who was trying to sell him a set of Victor Hugo on the instalment plan. Later Zabrini explained in court, "Sure I hit him with an iron pipe—but it was the soft end."

V-2 bombs were still bursting in London, and Winston Churchill was very much the prime minister, when he hailed a taxi in the Strand and asked to be driven to the British Broadcasting Corporation.

"Sorry, mister," said the cabbie. "Ye'll 'ave to get yourself another cab. Mr. Churchill is broadcastin' in thirty minutes and I wouldn't miss it for all the fares in London."

Churchill was so flattered that he pressed a pound note into the cabbie's hand. The latter looked at it in astonishment and came to a quick decision. "You're a bit of all right, sir," he exclaimed. " 'Op in, and to 'ell with Mr. Churchill."

A small hotel caught fire in the middle of the night. One guest was not yet asleep, so he got out quickly, and stood with the usual crowd of sensation-seekers, watching less fortunate guests run out, jump out, and be carried out by resolute firemen. He turned to the man beside him and observed smugly, "I don't see how people allow themselves to be panicked by a fire. Take me, for instance. I dressed carefully, put my valuables in my jacket, and emerged calmly. You see I even took time to put on my collar and tie."

The man addressed looked at him for the first time. "I presume," he said, "that you always appear publicly naked below the waist?"

A Back Bay society lady's idea for entertaining a ward of disabled soldiers in a Boston hospital was a speech on the evils of drink by an old battle-ax who had been shooting off her mouth on the subject since Carrie Nation wore diapers. The boys listened incredulously at first, and a bit sullenly, but brightened when the lady worked herself up to fever pitch and shrilled, "Before I would let a drop of vile liquor pass my lips, I—I—why, I'd commit adultery." From one end of the ward came a quiet voice, "Who wouldn't, lady?"

After two years in the Pittsburgh office of a big organization, a girl was transferred to the New York headquarters. The morning she reported at her new post, the big chief called her into his sanctum and said, "I hope you'll be happy here. The work will be practically the same as you were doing in the Pittsburgh office." "Okay," she replied. "Kiss me, and let's get started."

Lew Parker declares that his ancestors go back to Columbus. "In fact," he adds, "some of them even go back to Toledo."

Great-Great-Grandma Beebe studied the new-born babe with obvious satisfaction. "If my memory doesn't fail me," she cackled, "it's a boy."

A New Yorker was driving along a lonely New Hampshire road when he spied a lone farmer and stopped to check on his bearings.

Reassured, he observed casually, "That your farmhouse over there?" "Yup," said the farmer. "Only one in six miles on this road, mister."

"Six miles!" gasped the New Yorker. "It's mighty pretty country, but don't you get lonesome around here?"

"LONESOME!" snorted the native. "Lonesome, nothin'! Why, mister, on a clear day we can see Mt. Washington!"

Just as a Santa Fe train was pulling out of the station, a young man threw his bag on to the observation platform, and swung himself up over the handrail. He stood panting but triumphant as the train gathered speed.

An elderly party on the platform observed him with some scorn. "You young fellows don't keep yourselves in condition," he snorted. "Look at how done in you are! Why, when I was your age I could carry a cup of coffee in one hand, run half a mile, catch the 8:15 by the skin of my teeth, and still be as fresh as a daisy."

"You don't understand, pop," puffed the young man. "I missed this train at the *last* station."

The only hotel in town was so crowded that the famous author on his lecture tour was installed in the bridal suite. When he left, he forgot his umbrella. At the station, he figured he just about had time to go back for it. The room was locked when he got there, however, and a lovey-dovey couple within were making no apparent effort to keep their romancing a secret. "Whose ittle mouf is that?" cried the ecstatic bridegroom. "Yours," sighed his bride. Smack! "Whose ittle neck is that?" "Yours, honeybun." Smack! Smack! "Whose ittle gweat big eyes?" "Yours, all yours." Bedlam. . . .

The author could take no more of it. He rattled the doorknob loudly and hollered, "Hey you in there. When you get to an umbrella it's mine!"

There is a certain producer at MGM whose assaults on the English language have made history. In one of his humbler moments he announced, "I may not always be right, but I'm never wrong." Another time he told his yes-men, "I had a terrific idea in bed last night, boys —but I didn't like it." (It was of this studio that Philip Barry remarked, "The MGM lot is not a happy one.")

"Guilty or not guilty?" thundered the Judge. "Dunno," said the prisoner meekly. "I ain't heard the evidence yet."

The girl on the witness stand looked like something dreamed up by Varga, and Judge Timberwolf absentmindedly straightened his necktie and asked in dulcet tones, "Where were you, my dear, night before last?" "Entertaining a gentleman friend," she said demurely. "And where were you last night?" he persisted. "Entertaining another gentleman friend," she admitted. The judge was halfway off the bench as he whispered, "And where are you going to be tonight?" "Objection!" shouted the prosecuting attorney. "I asked her first!"

"Mighty big tip you handed that cloakroom attendant," commented Park. "It seemed only fair," said Tilford. "Look at the beautiful new coat she gave me."

A resident of Dallas was having a drink at a New York bar when a convivial next to him suggested "Have one on me." "That's right sportin' of you, pardner," said the Texan. "What state you hail from?" The stranger waved his arm expansively and declared, "From the best damn state in all the world." "Funny," frowned the man from Dallas. "You don't sound like no Texan to me."

The authoress of a current best seller very obviously considers herself an irresistible glamour girl, conveniently disregarding a formidable set of buck teeth. An ungallant soul at a literary tea created a furor by telling her, "I'll bet you're the only person in New York who can eat a tomato through a tennis racket."

In the days when Gene Fowler and Jack Barrymore were inseparable, sometimes on the wagon and sometimes not, they caused quite a commotion in a residential section of White Plains by driving up to a mansion at four in the morning in a New York taxicab and banging on the door until the nightshirted master of the establishment opened it. The temperature was about ten below zero, and the visitors were very cold and very noisy. "It's Fowler and Barrymore," the startled host called up to his wife. "Land's sake!" she exclaimed. "Are they sober?" "I'm not sure," reported the host, "but both of them are wearing the uniform of the New York Giants."

"Pop," said a boy of ten, "how do wars get started?" "Well, son," began Pop, "let us say that America quarreled with England—" "America is not quarreling with England," interrupted Mother. "Who said she was?" said Pop, visibly irritated. "I merely was giving the boy a hypothetical instance." "Ridiculous," snorted Mother. "You'll put all sorts of wrong ideas in his head." "Ridiculous nothing," countered Pop. "If he listens to you, he'll never have any ideas at all in his head." Just as the lamp-throwing stage approached, the son spoke up again: "Thanks, Mom. Thanks, Pop. I'll never have to ask how wars get started again."

At a rural crossroad in Canada there is a traffic sign which reads, "Take care which rut you use. You'll be in it for the next twenty miles."

A hopeful Kansan submitted to a Boston firm a poem entitled "Why Do I Live?" It was returned with a note reading, "We regret we cannot use your poem, but we can answer your question. It is because you mailed the poem to us instead of delivering it in person."

An English lord and his groom ran into each other head on, to their mutual astonishment, in one of the lower pits of Hell. "How now, master," said the groom. "What are you doing in these parts? I always thought that a man as generous and fair, and popular as you would go straight to Heaven!" "Ah, John," sighed the lord, "I was sent here because I cheated and defrauded my tenants and everybody else to pay the debts of that rascal, that apple of an old man's eye, my son. But you, John, a good fellow like you, why were you sent to Hell?" "For begetting that son," said the groom sadly.

"It's such a fine day," said the broker to his assistant, "that I think I'll go down to the club and shoot a round of golf." "I wish I was rich," the assistant said a little later to his secretary. "I wouldn't mind getting out into this sunshine once in a while myself." "Don't be a sap," the secretary told him. "How will old Poop-face know if you call for your wife and sneak off to the beach?"

The assistant thought this was an excellent suggestion. At his home, however, he had considerable difficulty getting the front door open; when he did force his way in, there was the boss, making violent love to his wife! The assistant gasped, stole silently out of the house, and paddled back to the office as fast as his little feet would carry him. "What happened?" said the secretary. "Didn't you go to the beach?" "What happened," echoed the assistant. "You and your fancy ideas! On account of you I darn near got fired!"

A Londoner, very correct and very superior, was being shown the sights of Ireland by a native courier. They included the Devil's Gorge, the Devil's Whirlpool, and the Devil's Bowl, and led the Englishman to drawl, "Old Nick seems to be an extremely important personage in Ireland." "Right you are," said the guide, "but like all the other landlords, he makes his home in England."

When the Florida real-estate boom was at its height, many an "investor" paid fabulous sums for property that usually was invisible under six feet of water. One victim ruefully surveyed his worthless acres, and made a beeline for the promoter who had sold it to him. "You faker," he shouted. "Didn't you tell me I could grow nuts on that property?" "I did not," said the promoter firmly. "I told you you could go nuts on it."

"What a hayseed," jeered the sophomore. "You must hail from the kind of hole where the entire population's chief amusement comes from traipsing to the station and watching the train go by."

"What train?" asked the freshman.

Somebody has just discovered what Scotchmen do with old razor blades. They shave with them.

Mogull came mooching back from the race track with his coat collar turned up despite the 80-degree weather. "What happened to me shouldn't happen to a dog," he reported. "I get a sure thing on the seventh race—a real long shot—65 to 1. So I bet two thousand dollars on the nose. My nag is a mile ahead at the last turn—the money is already in the bank—when suddenly he stumbles over something and pulls up lame. Curtains!"

"If anything like that happened to me," a friend sympathized, "I think I'd cut my throat." With a dramatic gesture, Mogull flung open his coat collar. "Look!" he commanded.

Mrs. Mitchum's eighteen-year-old daughter was as pretty as she was shy. She was blushing slightly as she came out of the parlor of the new Mitchum summer cottage. "Why did you leave it to me to greet the parson when he called?" she asked her mother. "Parson!" exclaimed Mrs. Mitchum. "Don't be silly. That was the doctor." Her daughter was visibly relieved. "That's all right then," she said. "I *thought* he was a little bit familiar for a parson."

A country editor tried to persuade the local tycoon to give him a full-page advertisement for his Christmas supplement. "Where does your paper go?" inquired the dubious tycoon. The editor declared, "It goes from Maine to California, from the Great Lakes to the Gulf, and if you don't give me that ad pretty quick it is going straight to hell."

A writer in London says a report has reached those parts to the effect that Hollywood brides now keep the bouquets and throw away the bridegrooms. I wonder if he's heard about the starlet named Mary, who had a little wolf, and fleeced him white as snow?

"School facilities, Mr. Dillingham?" repeated the real-estate agent. "I assure you, sir, that there is a big modern school within a stone's throw of this beautiful estate."

Mr. Dillingham had good cause to believe the agent, for at this precise moment a stone the size of a canteloupe hit him squarely over the left ear.

A favorite food of the Hawaiians is called "poi." It is prepared, says the dictionary, from the taro root, whatever that is, pounded to a paste and allowed to ferment.

At any rate, a tourist in a newly opened Honolulu hash house demanded a portion of this poi as an experiment. "What kind would you be wanting?" asked the waiter. "What kind would you be having?" replied the tourist. "Let's see," said the waiter, counting on his fingers. "We got apple, lemon, huckleberry, an' peach."

Fibber McGee claims he's been getting laughs for twenty years with the story of the hillbilly wife whose consuming passion was jealousy for her virile husband. In an attic one day she came across the first mirror she ever had seen. She peered into it, shook her head, and muttered, "So that's the ugly old hag he's been running around with!"

A Georgia farmer told his hired hand to drive into town for some supplies, raged when he showed up a full hour later than he should have. "No, sir! I warn't wastin' time at the saloon at all," he protested. "It's just that I picked up Parson Abernathy down the road about three miles and from then on them pesky mules couldn't understand a word I said."

Two partners took a day off to shoot a round of golf. On the third tee, one partner suddenly exclaimed, "My God, I think I forgot to lock the cash box." "So what?" said the other. "We're both here, ain't we?"

A stranger accosted the first man he met in a little Scotch village and asked, "Do you know where Jock MacGregor lives?" "Never heard o' him," averred the native. "Could it be he has a nickname o' one sort or another?" "It seems to me," mused the stranger, "that I've heard him referred to as the tightest, meanest, most blasphemous old coot North of Aberdeen." "Ach, why did ye no say so in the first place," said the Scot. "That's me!"

"Dis am de thermos bottle mah wife done gib me for Christmas," said Sambo proudly. "It kin keep coffee blazin' hot all day. Or it kin keep lemonade ice cold de same len'th o' time." "Mah goodness," marveled his friend, "how do it know which to do?"

A famous delicatessen in New York has a sign prominently displayed on the wall that reads, "We make every kind of sandwich in the world. Just ask for it." Late one night a prankster demanded a whale sandwich. The waiter stalled and said, "I'll have to speak to the boss." He came back after a hurried consultation and reported, "The boss says he's damned if he'll cut up a whale just for one sandwich."

STOP!
DON'T READ
TOO MANY
JOKES AT ONE TIME.
THEY'RE FUNNIER IN SMALL DOSES

FARMER Thomas' neighbor gave him a sow for his birthday and it wasn't long before he thought it would be nice to have a litter of little pigs to go with it. A farmer who lived three miles away offered him the use of his boar for $2.00. Farmer Thomas put his sow into a wheelbarrow and pushed it the necessary three miles under the hot sun. The next morning he came down expecting to find a lot of little pigs gambolling about, but found the sow in solitary grandeur.

"No wonder," said the man at the Fair two weeks later when he heard about this experience. "What do you expect from a $2.00 boar? I've got a prize-winning boar at my place fifteen miles from yours that I will let you use for $10.00." The next day Farmer Thomas put his sow in the wheelbarrow and pushed it fifteen miles. "This time I am sure to have some little pigs," he told himself, but the next morning he was disappointed again.

A few weeks later he read in the paper that Joshua Spriggins, who lived thirty miles away, owned the national champion boar, great-grandson of Blueboy, and offered the use of same for $50.00. The persistent Farmer Thomas loaded his sow into the wheelbarrow again and trudged the fifty miles in dogged silence. The next morning he woke up in a dither of excitement. "I'll bet there'll be twenty little pigs around this time," he told his wife, and rushed down to the sty. He was wrong again. There wasn't a little pig in sight, but the sow was sitting in the wheelbarrow.

When a doctor told a famous actress: "You must stop taking sleeping pills or they'll become an unbreakable habit," she replied angrily, "Don't be silly. I've been taking those pills every night for twenty years, and they're not a habit yet."

Arthur Kober is distinctly an extrovert, but one night he had a dream that he thinks has Freudian connotations. He dreamed that he was marooned on a desert island with nothing to eat and nothing to do. He hadn't seen a soul in months—especially a girl—when suddenly a canoe came heading his way and out of it stepped the South American bombshell, Miss Carmen Miranda. She wasn't wearing many clothes, but she had on the typical Miranda headdress. With a hoarse cry of joy, Kober seized her in his arms and threw her to the ground. Then he ate every bit of food on her hat.

Orton Tewson tells the story of an old lady in a tiny Yorkshire parish who lay dying. She said sadly to her husband, "Eh, lad, I wonder whatever the puir bairns will do after I be gone." "Get along wi' thy dyin', lass," replied he soothingly. "I will mind t' bairns."

Joe Kennedy reminded a business college class, "Almost anybody can lose his shirt in Wall Street if he's got enough capital to start with and the proper inside information."

In New Orleans an author told James M. Cain that book critics were simply weird in their ignorance and often confused themselves with God. He added hastily, "The confusion is unjustified."

In New York a hopeful author visited Harrison Smith to see what had happened to a manuscript he had submitted several months previously. Mr. Smith was cleaning his desk and said, while he continued with his cleaning, "I am quite sure your novel never was brought to my attention." The author cried, "There it is." The absent-minded Mr. Smith had just thrown the manuscript into the wastebasket.

The English barmaid was a flirtatious piece, and the tall, sunburned Texan private was right down her alley. The MP had left the bar for a moment, and the barmaid cuddled up to the Texan, and murmured, "Here's your chance, big boy." "You said it," agreed the private enthusiastically—and drank the MP's beer.

Ethel Barrymore tells about the time Modjeska, the tempestuous Polish actress, came to London to take the feminine lead in a new play, opposite her father. The fact that Modjeska was virtually unknown in London didn't stop her from staging a series of tantrums and hysterical fits. Finally the elder Barrymore lost his temper completely and shouted, "Woman, shut up! *I* am the star of this company." "You dare say that to me?" she screamed. "Me, the great Modjeska?" "Let me remind you, madame," he answered, "that I am a Barrymore. Here in London, the people do not know whether you are a woman or a tooth powder."

An excitable housewife called her husband, who was in the midst of an important business conference, and babbled "John, that nasty butcher just told me to go to hell. What do you advise?" The husband suggested, "Do it," and hung up.

The proprietor of an East Side dry-goods emporium left the store, with some misgivings, in the hands of a new clerk while he went out for a bite of lunch and a stogie. When he came back, the clerk proudly announced that he had sold a coolie coat in his absence. The pleased proprietor opened the drawer of the cash register, and then let out a wild cry of anguish. "Ninety-eight cents!" he screamed. "Mawrus, you didn't sell that gudgeous coolie coat for *ninety-eight cents*?" "Did I do wrong?" said the clerk. "I looked first at the tag." "It was ninety-eight *dollars*, you shlemiel," groaned the boss, "not ninety-eight cents." However, his lunch had been good, and he soon relented. "Let this be a lesson to you, Mawrus," he said. "And dun't feel too bad about it. We made fifteen cents' profit anyhow."

The clerk had a slightly happier experience the very next day. "I sold a man a pair of brown shoes for six dollars," he said. "He only had a dollar forty with him, so I took that as a deposit." "You incurable fool,"

lamented the boss. "He'll never come back!"

"He'll come back all right," said the now-confident clerk. "I gave him two left shoes."

*

"Last night," reported Private Higgins, "I finally persuaded my girl to say 'yes.'" "Congrats," said his buddy. "When's the wedding?" "Wedding?" said Higgins. "What wedding?"

*

After his fourteenth highball, Jackson staggered out of Clancy's bar, and crashed head-on into the corner lamppost. Rubbing his forehead sadly, he next tripped over the fire hydrant. Reeling across the sidewalk, he somersaulted down the steps of Mrs. Sullivan's basement, and landed in a bloody heap. "T'hell with it," he told himself as he curled up for a good sleep. "I might as well stay here 'till the parade passes."

*

An English appraisal of the American character (from a travel journal published in 1830):

"An American farmer brought a cart full of pigeons to Philadelphia market on a day there happened to be a glut of them, and could find no purchasers. He offered them at half price. Still no purchasers. Not caring to load his cart back again, he then offered to give them away, but the people, supposing they must be stolen, would not have them. He then drove his cart on and dropped three or four every ten yards, but somebody always picked them up, bawled, 'Mister, you are losing your pigeons,' and threw them back again in his cart. Mortified, the man stopped his horse, and leaned back, pretending to be asleep. Instantly, man, woman and child set to work and stole every one of his pigeons."

*

A reader of society columns couldn't understand why so many stalwart gentlemen from Tiflis and Batum seemed to be princes. George Jean Nathan explained it. "In Georgia," he pointed out, "a prince is a man who rates the title of 'mister' in any other country."

Daring young rips at Rector's whispered the story of the young couple who registered at a tiny upstate inn. Seeing that they had no baggage the careful proprietor demanded to see their wedding license. The man fished in his pocket and could find only a hunting permit. He folded it up, thrust it in the proprietor's hands, and demanded his room and bath.

Ten minutes later the proprietor banged loudly on the couple's door and hollered, "If ye ain't done it, don't do it! 'Tain't fer it!"

The game of fitting odd words into sentences continues merrily among the punsters. One grim party produced the following horrible examples:

SOVIET: Dinner was ready soviet.

CADILLAC: A cadillac mean if you pull its tail.

BOLL WEEVIL: After the boll weevil all go home.

LOQUACIOUS: She bumped into me and I told her to loquacious going.

Forty miles out of Chicago on the Super-Chief, Mrs. Lapidus let out a wail. "If only we had the grand piano with us, Papa!" "On a trip like this, why do you need the grand piano?" asked Lapidus. "Because," she explained, "that is where I left the tickets."

A business man grumbled to his secretary, "This has been the darndest day! Everybody is certainly getting dumb. I've asked twenty people what time it is—and every single one of them has given me a different answer!"

Even more baffled was a banker who asked an elevator man, "Can you tell me the time?" and was answered, "Do you mean *now?*"

"Horse sense," Herbert Swope decided after a rocky day at the Tropical Park track, "is the thing a horse has that keeps him from betting on people."

A beautiful Hollywood model was upbraiding her young brother because he was continually in debt. "Look at how well I'm doing," she protested. "Why can't you follow my example?" "You don't seem to understand, sis," he said, "that it's just what's making you rich that's making me poor!"

A junk dealer was driving his dilapidated horse and wagon across the Triborough Bridge and was horrified to discover that he had to pay a twenty-five cent toll. "A Rulls-Royce yet they think I am," he muttered angrily. When he returned the following day the old horse was sitting in the wagon, and the junk dealer was pulling it.

"Where's your quarter toll?" asked the guard.

"Dun't come to me," said the dealer. "Esk de driver."

Friedman was aghast when he walked into his apartment and found his wife Jezebel walking on the ceiling. "Hello," she said calmly. "What do you mean, 'hello'?" he ejaculated. "What are you doing walking on that ceiling? Don't you know it's against the laws of gravity?" There was a terrible crash as Jezebel fell to the floor. Gingerly rubbing the ample spot upon which she had fallen, she looked at him in a rage and blurted, "You had to open that big mouth of yours, didn't you?"

"Battleships?" boasted the British tar. "Why, matey, our flagship is so big it takes the admiral an hour to cruise around the deck in a limousine." "So what?" sneered the American bluejacket. "The galley of our flagship is so big the cook has to go through the Irish stew in a submarine to see if the potatoes are done!"

An English author broke off his lecture tour in Iowa. "I never minded people looking at their watches while I talked," he told his agent, "but out there they shake them."

Edgar Bergen made his radio debut in 1936 when he managed to engineer an audition for the guest spot on the Rudy Vallée program. The sponsor declared audibly that anybody who thought a ventriloquist could hold a radio audience's attention was screwy as a bird dog. Bergen was so nervous that he almost dropped his precious Charlie McCarthy and muffed several lines in the script. The sponsor chortled derisively. An assistant waved a copy of the script at Bergen and said, "Here's your place." Bergen nodded and the assistant moved away. "Hey," yelled Charlie, "let me have a gander at that script." The young man wheeled about and unthinkingly thrust the script before the wooden dummy's eyes. The sponsor stared at the spectacle, muttered "I'll be damned," and ordered, "Make out a contract for that guy."

A man with a lot of baggage stood cussing on the Albuquerque platform. "S'matter?" asked the station agent. "I had to get that Super-Chief," was the explanation. "Averaged seventy an hour for ninety miles and busted two springs—and then I miss it by a single minute." "My goodness," commented the agent. "Anybody seeing the way you're carrying on would think you'd missed it by an hour!"

A voluptuous blonde threw her full-length ermine wrap over the back of a chair. "I picked this up for a song," she explained. "Really," commented Joan Davis, "It looks more like an overture to me."

Mrs. Chase made the mistake of leaving the baby in her husband's care while she went into the library to pay the month's bills. Mr. Chase buried himself behind his newspaper, and forgot all about the baby until he heard a series of thumps, followed by a horrendous wail. Clearly, the baby had fallen down the stairs. "Martha," called Mr. Chase excitedly. "Come quick! Junior just took his first forty-eight steps!"

A patron of the Automat watched a man at his table pour eight spoonfuls of sugar into his coffee, and then start drinking without stirring it. "Why don't you stir that coffee?" he asked. The other regarded him coldly and answered, "Who likes it sweet?"

The landlord eyed his prospective tenant coldly. "I must remind you," he said, "that I will not tolerate children, dogs, cats, or parrots. And no piano playing. And no radio. Is that clear?"

"Yes, sir," said the tenant meekly. "But I think you ought to know that my fountain pen scratches a little."

Relatives brought poor old Mr. Lewisheim to a psychoanalyst when he refused to take off his heavy winter overcoat straight through a ten-day hot spell that broke all records at the weather bureau. By the time the doctor got him, Mr. Lewisheim's condition could be described as high. He sat huddled in a corner, clutching the heavy coat frantically about him. "I dassn't open it," he explained after the psychoanalyst had won his confidence. "I got three butterflies in there and if I open the coat they'll escape." The doctor put him under an anaesthetic, and before he regained consciousness, pinned three dead butterflies to a card. "See," he told Lewisheim, "your butterflies are gone. No reason to wear that coat again until December." Everything seemed fine, but a week later the despairing relatives brought Lewisheim back, wrapped tighter than ever in his heavy ulster. "What now?" asked the doctor sternly. "You saw for yourself that the butterflies were gone. What's the point of still crouching in that great coat?" "I gotta," whispered Mr. Lewisheim. "If I open it, how do I know three brand-new butterflies won't fly in?"

A doctor was sound asleep in the middle of the night when a scratching noise at the back door awakened him. Upon investigation, he found a coal-black cocker spaniel with a badly cut foot. Half amused, half indignant, he carried the pooch to his laboratory, poured iodine on the cut, and bandaged the paw neatly. The dog licked his face, and limped off.

A week or so later, the doctor was awakened again by a similar noise. He arose with an angry exclamation and pulled open the door. The black cocker was back, 100 per cent sound, but he had with him another dog whose paw was injured.

Believe it or not, one and the same man, who wisely signed himself "A. Nonymous," included the following three gems in a single contribution:

1. Suzy Smith put on her skates upon the ice to frisk; her friends thought she was slightly nuts her little *. 2. Mary had an Ingersoll but swallowed it one day; she rushed to get some epsom salts to pass the time away. 3. Weasel Willie, mean as hell, dropped his sister down the well; his mother sighed while drawing water, "Gosh, it's tough to raise a daughter."

A Hollywood agent came home unexpectedly and caught one of his biggest clients making violent love to his wife. The agent's denunciations made no particular impression on the guilty client. "Stop sounding like a B picture, Joe," he said. "Let's treat this situation like adults. You love your wife and so do I. Let's play one game of gin rummy—and the winner gets her." The agent considered for a moment and agreed. "Okay," he said slowly, "but what do you say we play for a nickel a point on the side just to make it interesting?"

At a recent stockholders' meeting of the United States Steel Corporation, Chairman Olds introduced various officials of the company, and was just preparing to take up the day's business when one stockholder in the rear got up and yelled, "And who are you and what do you do for this company?" "I'm your chairman," laughed Olds, not in the least disconcerted. "Of course you know the duties of a chairman. I'd say he was roughly the equivalent of parsley on a platter of fish."

Every light suddenly went out at the Hawkins place and Pa and Ma went down in the cellar to investigate. "Put your hand on thet there wire, Maw," commanded Pa, "and tell me if you feel anything." "Nothin' at all," reported Ma. "Good," said Pa. "Now just don't touch the other one, or ye'll probably drop dead."

A Winston editor tried hard to cheer a disconsolate author recently. "What you should do," he counselled, "is climb out of your lonely shell, get married, take a nice penthouse in town, give parties, have children and dogs and things." "If you don't mind," groaned the author, "I think I'll commit suicide."

Some book publishers trust each other almost as much as dress manufacturers. A group of them was gathered at luncheon at the Yale Club the other day, and laughed uproariously at a timely witticism. A competitor sat near by viewing them anxiously. "Only one thing can be *that* funny," he muttered to his companion. "I bet one of those so-and-so's has stolen my best author."

The shortest drama review on record was turned in by the critic of a London gazette. The play was called *Dreadful Night*. The critic's complete comment was "exactly." . . .

Charles Frohman imported a light English drawing-room comedy that had delighted London audiences for a solid year. New York, however, would have none of it. A week after the opening, the author cabled, "How is it going?" Frohman cabled back, "It's gone." . . .

An aspiring playwright sent a script to J. M. Barrie for

criticism. Barrie read it and wrote, "My dear Sir: I have glanced over your play. Oh my dear Sir!" . . .

Jimmy Cannon once alleged that a play was so bad, "the audience hissed the ushers." . . .

Oscar Wilde saw the first night of one of his infrequent fiascos, and buttonholed a critic on the way out. "I hope you noticed," he said, "that the play itself was a great success. It was the audience that was a failure."

You must have heard about the man who discovered a tombstone on which was engraved, "Here lies a lawyer and an honest man," and whose comment was, "Ground sure must be scarce in this cemetery. Imagine burying two men in a single grave!" And the client who called his attorney to explain a predicament in which he found himself. "Cheer up," counselled the attorney. "They can't put you in jail for that." "Maybe so," said the client, "but I'm speaking from the jail now."

Mrs. Schlamm came home from an afternoon of shopping and discovered her husband in the act of packing a suitcase. "Where do you think you're going?" she asked. "Chicago," he said, defiantly. "I just read in the paper that men have gotten so scarce out there that women are paying them $2.00 to take them home and be nice to them."

Mrs. Schlamm nodded her head up and down a few times without saying anything. A few minutes later Mr. Schlamm found that his wife also was throwing her belongings into a valise. "Where are you bound for?" he asked. "I am going to Chicago too," said Mrs. Schlamm. "I just want to see how you are going to manage to live on $4.00 a month."

A famous comedian held up production of a motion-picture for three days because of a "persistent cough." "Listen," the director shouted over the phone. "There are just two kinds of coughs: drunken and the one you haven't got."

Mr. Whoosh, master plumber, observed his new gilt sign, "Whoosh & Son," with keen satisfaction. "Now that you are a member of the firm, my boy," he told his son, "I must remind you again that one quality a plumber must have above all others is tact. Plumbers have to fix leaks in very strange places sometimes. I will never forget, for instance, the time I went in to fix the pipes in a bathroom in a Park Avenue penthouse. There was a beautiful lady sitting in the tub! I remembered about tact, however, and quickly said, 'Pardon me, sir,' and walked out without quickening my pace at all."

The son promised to remember. A few weeks later he reported to his father, "Pop, your little lecture on tact stood me in good stead this morning. I had to fix a break in the pipe in the bridal suite of a big hotel on Fifth Avenue. When I walked in, I saw that the couple who were occupying the suite hadn't gotten up yet. I didn't say a word until I had stopped the leak. Then, on the way out, I simply nodded my head and said, 'Good day, gentlemen.'"

The year that the Olympic swimming meet was held in Los Angeles, according to a local historian, one of the diving champs saw a chance to make a little pin money by doubling for a star in a spectacular shot. The day he appeared to do his stunt, the assistant director had forgotten to have the pool filled. "Hey, you goon," yelled the champ. "How do you expect me to do my dive when there's no water in the pool?" "How do you like that?" exclaimed the assistant director to the world at large. "Five minutes on the set and he gets temperamental."

"What are ye doin' ridin' down the high street on a woman's bicycle?" cried Jock.

"I went off on a picnic with a bonnie lassie this mornin'," explained Hamish. "On the moor I threw me arms about her and kissed her fer a muckle. She liked it. She liked it verra much. In fact, she suddenly said, 'Hamish, I'll give ye anything ye like.' So I took the bicycle."

Mrs. Hotstuff breezed into a butcher shop and gazed down her elongated proboscis at the clerk. "I'll have two dozen chops," she said, "and see that you make them lean." "Yes, ma'am," said the clerk meekly. "To the left or the right?"

"What," asks Viewer-with-alarm Warren of Boston, "will the short skirt be up to next?"

Abbott and Costello were in Baltimore unexpectedly one night, and sought a room at the Belvedere Hotel. "All I've got available," said the clerk sorrowfully, "is the bridal suite. Do you, Abbott, take it?" "I do," said Abbott. "Do you, Costello, take it too?" "I do," echoed Costello. The clerk thrust the register at them and declared, "I now pronounce you room and bath."

A reporter interviewed William Jennings Bryan at an early stage of the silver-tongued orator's career. "Put this in your paper, son," said Bryan. "A man simply can't make a million dollars honestly." Years later, when Bryan had salted away quite a pile in one activity and another, the reporter, now an editor, said slyly, "Remember what you told me about rich men in this very hotel long ago?" "Certainly," boomed Bryan. "I said, 'A man simply can't make two million dollars honestly.'"

The sons and daughters of Mr. Bauer held a conference to discuss the wayward habits of their aging parent. His oldest son came to Bauer with the concensus of the meeting. "Pop," he said, "we have decided that a man of your age simply has no right to go out with young chorus girls so often. You're absolutely ruining your health. I want you to promise me that you will go to the doctor and ask him just how often he will permit you to take out these chickens."

The old man reluctantly consented and visited his doctor the very next day. When he came back, the son was waiting for him. "Well," he said, "what did the doctor say?" The old man scratched his head in a rather perplexed manner and said, "I'm not sure, my boy. How many times a week is semiannual?"

When they pulled Arthur Godfrey out of a wrecked automobile, he explained, "I taught my girl how to drive this car, but I forgot to show her how to aim it."

MacKinlay Kantor was flying over Canada one sunny morning when the man next to him suddenly inquired,

"Say, did that Dionne fellow ever have any more quin-tuplets?" "Certainly not," said Kantor. "I knew it," maintained the other triumphantly. "I always said that guy was a flash in the pan."

"I can't tell you how long I have labored on this manuscript," the aspiring writer told the producer, "polishing a scene here, adding a line there, eliminating scenes, and adding new characters." "What a pity," said the producer, handing it back to him. "All work—and no play."

The *Wall Street Journal* tells about an old Nevada judge whose methods of doling out justice were just a wee bit arbitrary. One morning he opened court with the following announcement, "Gents, I have in hand a check—a bribe you could call it, I guess—from the plaintiff for $10,000 and another from the defendant for $15,000. I propose to return $5000 to the defendant, and then will decide the case strictly on its merits."

Walter Marquess accompanied Ring Lardner to an annual Homecoming game in the days when Illinois boasted the galloping Red Grange and a crack student battery of artillery. Just before game-time, the first salute gun was fired as Governor Small entered his box. Lardner jumped from his seat, and demanded, "What was that?" "For the governor," explained Marquess. Just then the second gun blasted away. "My God," cried Lardner. "They missed him."

Harrison Cousins was working late at the plant when they handed him a telegram. It read "Your wife just gave birth to her third baby girl." Pinned to the message was a printed form: "If you want a boy, call Western Union."

The box-office treasurer of a vaudeville theatre in St. Paul sold a ticket for a matinee to a man with one of those faces that haunt you for days after you've seen it. He was startled, therefore, to see the same man come back a couple of minutes later and buy another ticket for the same show. When the character appeared to purchase a third ducat, the treasurer said, "I know it's none of my business, but I suppose you realize that this is the third ticket you have bought for the same show." "Of course I realize it," said the little man with a sigh, "but when I handed the other tickets to the man at the door he tore them up."

When it comes to telling Jewish stories, Harry Hershfield and Lou Holtz are just about in a class by themselves. I've heard both of them tell the following story, so propose to split the credit for it between them.

Shapiro lost his last dollar at the Jamaica Race Track and came to his old friend Rosenblatt for a job. "It ain't like I had nothing to offer you," he said modestly. "I think most of Woodmere would agree I am positively the greatest salesman in town." "This I do not propose to argue with you," conceded Roenblatt. "We don't need anybody in our regular line just now, but I just bought a hundred dozen boxes of cigars which maybe a great salesman like you could turn over at six or seven dollars a box."

"Nothing to it," said Shapiro, but when friend after friend sampled his cigars and promptly booted him out of their offices, he lost heart. Finally he dumped the boxes back on Rosenblatt's desk and said, "Something I got to tell you. I ain't the best salesman in town after all. I'm the second best. The fellow who sold you those cigars—he's the best!"

Nunnally Johnson's capsule definition of a motion-picture preview: "A place where four or five men, each making $4000 or $5000 a week, go to watch a pimply-faced kid write 'It stinks' on a card."

A city man asked a farmer "How far would you say it was to Flemington?" "Wal," calculated the farmer, "It's 24,992 miles the direction you're headin'; 'bout seven if you turn 'round."

A book salesman imbibed a couple too many at a literary cocktail party in the Times Square area. He engaged in a long discussion about women with an editor from Lippincott's, and when the party was over, left with his friend to settle the question once and for all.

The next thing he remembers, a conductor was crying out, "Next stop, Philadelphia." The salesman put down his Scotch and soda on the table and clapped a hand to his head. "Philadelphia!" he marveled. "Good grief, I thought this was a lunch wagon."

The town pest met Harry Maule returning from the lake with a fine mess of salmon and observed, "Been fishin', ain't ye?" "By cricky, you're right," agreed Harry. "What'd ye use fer bait?" asked the pest. "Chewing tobacco," declared Harry. "Never heard o' nothin' like that bein' used fer bait," scoffed the pest. "How'd ye use it?"

"Well," explained Harry, "you just put it on the hook. The fish snaps it and retreats. Then when he comes up to the surface to spit, you conk him over the head with your pole."

A well-known citizen of San José met his ex-wife at a cocktail party, and, warmed by the libations, suggested that they have another go at connubial bliss. "Over my dead body," said the lady haughtily. "My error," said the erstwhile spouse. "I see you haven't changed a bit."

Somebody complained of the cold to S. J. Perelman. "Go to Mexico," advised the famous japester. "It may be Chile there today, but it's hot tamale."

A crotchety old buzzard stamped into a country doctor's office, brandished his cane, and wheezed "You're a danged old fraud! I came to you in 1904 to cure a cough, and you sent me a bill for three dollars." "I cured you, didn't I?" said the doctor angrily. "Cured me! That's rich, that is," blustered the old man. "Look at me! I'm sneezing again."

Ione Shriber was a house guest of the one and only Gypsy Rose Lee. She noticed that the bath towels there were luxuriantly beautiful, covered with elaborately embroidered flowers. "They were a wedding present from my first marriage," explained Gypsy. "They are wonderful," exclaimed Mrs. Shriber. "Sure they are," agreed Gypsy. "But Jeez, what a price to pay for a couple of bath towels."

In London Stanley Rinehart went to a tennis match and sat next to one of those typical Englishmen fully equipped with walrus mustache and monocle. The man turned to him suddenly and said, "You're an American, aren't you? I wonder if you know a chap out there named Smith." Rinehart doubted that he did. "Rum fellow," continued the Englishman. "Had a shooting box next to mine. Ran off with somebody else's wife. Worse still, I saw him shoot a pheasant on the ground. It was coming toward him, too."

An irascible Hollywood producer had fired a half-dozen high-powered advertising managers in four days. The newest victim presented his suggested lay-out with much trepidation. "This picture," was his headline, "combines the poetry of Shakespeare, the suspense of Poe, the wit of Voltaire, and the plot mastery of Dumas. More than an epic, greater than the Bible, it will give you a thrill that you will remember constantly for the rest of your life."

The producer studied the "ad" for a moment, chewed his cigar, and then slapped the desk vigorously. "That's more like it," he exclaimed happily. "Just simple facts. No overstatement!"

A country librarian was trying to find a sweet old lady a nice book to read. She finally offered her one about a cardinal. "But I'm not interested in religion," complained the old lady. The librarian laughed. "You don't understand," she said. "This is about a bird." The old lady continued to shake her head. "I am not interested in his private life either," she said firmly.

The only passenger in the elevator was a redheaded sailor. The pretty girl operator called "Up! Up! Anybody going up? *Please*, won't somebody go up?"

In the waiting room for expectant fathers at the Medical Center, Mr. Hargreave, awaiting news of his first-born, was charging up and down like a caged lion. Suddenly he stopped short in his tracks and exclaimed in some wonder, "I don't know why I should be so upset. After all, it's only my wife."

The new county school superintendent liked to throw his weight around and fell into the disconcerting habit of popping suddenly into a classroom while it was in session to inspect the proceedings. He decided that one classroom that he visited was far too noisy and, grabbing the tallest boy by the scruff of the neck, marched him off to the principal's office. "I'll teach you to make all that racket while class is in session," he thundered. "You just stand there in that corner for a while." About twenty minutes later, a delegation from the classroom appeared before him. "Mr. Jones," said the spokesman. "Now that you've taken our teacher away from us, can we have the rest of the morning off?"

Driving from one coast to the other, Harry Von Zell said that he knew the very minute that he got within range of Hollywood. All the road signs read, "Soft shoulders and dangerous curves ahead."

Freshman Boles shrieked with dismay when he heard that his shirt had been sent to the laundry. "Do you realize," he groaned, "that the entire history of the Roman Empire was on the cuff of that shirt?"

Five-year-old Michael was poring through an old copy of a book about the Christian martyrs filled with highly colored and lurid illustrations. When he came to a reproduction of the famous picture of the Christians being thrown to the lions in Nero's huge amphitheatre, he burst into tears. "My little Michael is so sensitive," boasted his mother to a visitor. "He is already conscious of the injustice of this world and the needless sufferings inflicted on fellow humans by barbarians." Michael continued to sob and pointed to one lion prowling all by himself in the left-hand corner of the picture. "Look at that poor lion over there," he sobbed. "He hasn't got a single Christian."

I once came home from Nassau aboard a vessel that was completing one of those fourteen-day, all-expenses-paid cruises of the West Indies. The night before we docked in New York was a "gala"— toy balloons, noise-makers, confetti—and, as a special treat, caviar added to the menu.

At the next table sat a very fat, pleasant-faced lady who obviously had never eaten caviar before. She planked a heaping tablespoonful on her plate, and added an equally large portion of grated onions when another waiter stopped by her. She mixed the caviar and onions very carefully, and spread them on a piece of black bread.

All of us waited impatiently for her verdict. She chewed in silence for a moment, and then shook her head knowingly. "So dot's caviar," she declared. "It tastes just like onions to me!"

Three privates in a dugout were whiling away some idle moments in a hot pinochle game. Rifkind had just essayed a bold bid of "500" when a stray shell whizzed by and took his head off just as clean as a whistle. His two companions were stunned for a moment. Then one climbed over the debris and looked at the decapitated man's hand. "You know, Al," he said, "I think he would have made it."

The late Lord Birkenhead, famous lawyer and after-dinner speaker, did not always see eye-to-eye with the judge before whom he was appearing. During an important trial at Liverpool, the judge demanded angrily, "Are you trying to teach me law, Sir?" Birkenhead replied sweetly, "I never attempt the impossible, m'lud."

Murphy had a clock whose chimes rang so loudly that neighbors six blocks away complained to the police. Murphy, however, slept blissfully through all the racket. For twenty years the chimes never missed a quarter-hour. Then one night, just before eleven, something went wrong with the mechanism and the clock was silent at the hour. Murphy awoke with a start, and jumped to his feet like a cat. "What happened?" he bellowed. "Who made that unholy noise?"

"You better give me a raise, Mr. Harper," his assistant told him. "Three other companies are after me." "A likely story," said Mr. Harper. "What companies?" "Light, Water, and Gas," said the assistant.

"If you refuse me," vowed the ardent swain on bended knee, "I shall die." She refused him, and seventy-two years later he died.

Dick Tregaskis had only had two lunches that day and he gazed with undisguised envy at a big sirloin steak that had just been put in front of his friend, Ward Greene. "Don't tell me," pleaded Tregaskis, "that you are going to eat that huge steak alone?" "No," said Greene, tucking his napkin carefully under his chin. "With potatoes."

A lieutenant in an occupied capital of Europe summoned a corporal and growled, "What's this I hear about your being so drunk last night that you pushed a wheelbarrow through the British Embassy?"

"You ought to know, sir," answered the corporal. "You were in the wheelbarrow."

The charges against Mulligan were highway robbery, rape, and the murder of eleven policemen. The slickest criminal lawyer in town offered to defend him for a down payment of $3000. "I wouldn't pay no lawyer $3000," shouted Mulligan. "Okay," said the criminal lawyer. "Get somebody else to defend you. He'll only charge you $1000, and you won't even have to pay that. Your heirs will."

A man who owned a house in the east sixties decided he was tired of it and asked "Cannonball" Gans, the famous realtor, to sell it for him. The following Sunday he read the "ad" Gans had worked up on the house in the *Times* real-estate section. Then he read it again. Then he called up Gans. "Cannonball," he said. "I've decided not to sell. That ad of yours convinced me that this is the kind of house I've been looking for all my life."

Robert Malloy, author of *Bride's Way*, inquires if anybody remembers the Irishman who wrote home to his brother, "America sure is a wonderful, wonderful place. Here I am pulling down the Lutheran Church and getting $10.00 a day for it."

When Howard Dietz was elected vice-president of MGM, he cancelled an order to send out a publicity note. Asked why, he explained modestly, "Everybody thinks I'm president."

Charles Morton of the *Atlantic Monthly* revives the story of the group of writers who were discussing the ideal opening for a commercially successful piece of fiction. They agreed that the first paragraph should contain (1) sex, (2) high life and big money, and (3) an unconventional situation. On that basis, one of them contrived this unbeatable beginning: "Damn it," said the Duchess to the King, "take your hand off my leg."

A mill that specialized in parachute silk was caught with a huge inventory on V-J Day. The alert plant manager promptly began converting his stock into thousands and thousands of sheer, irresistible ladies' unmentionables. Just before the first shipment was sent to market an added feature was discovered for which, it was decided, no extra charge would be levied.

Across the seat of each garment was printed, "Count ten before you pull the rip cord."

Clancy wandered backstage between the acts of a musical revue and innocently started to enter a room clearly marked "Chorus girls' dressing room. Positively no admittance." A watchman nabbed him in the act. "Can't you read?" he hollered, pointing to the sign. "Who's shmokin'?" asked Clancy.

One of Irvin Cobb's most popular Negro stories concerned a little wisp of a man who suddenly startled the community by joining in wedlock the fattest and most truculent old harridan in the county. The ill-matched pair settled in a cabin some seven miles from town, but a fortnight later came driving into Frankfort in a wagon containing all their household effects.

"Hello there, Mose," cried the postmaster. "Where are you going with all that plunder?" "I'se movin' into town, Mist' John," answered Mose. "I'se rented a little house by the L and N depot." "But I thought you liked living in the country," said the postmaster. "I used to lak it," said Mose. "I used to lak it powerful. But my wife she don't lak the country. And yere lately I've tuck notice, Mist' John, dat we'en my wife don't lak a thing, I just natchelly hates it."

There is another Cobb story that remains popular, its typically leisurely tempo offering a welcome contrast to the slam-bang, wisecracking school of humor that characterizes the radio programs of today. This one's setting is the funeral of the town's leading merchant. The procession, on its way to the merchant's last resting place, passed a cabin where an ancient couple resided. The pair in question were engaged that afternoon in the pursuit of their favorite occupation of doing nothing whatsoever. The old man was stretched on the earth with his back against the wall of the house

and facing the road. His wife, in a rickety armchair, was facing in the other direction, massaging her front teeth with a snuff stick. Presently she spoke. "What's that I hear a-passin'?" "It's Jim Combs' fune'l just goin' by." "Much of a turnout?" "Biggest I ever done seen in these parts," he answered. "More than twenty hacks and waggins, looks like, and a whole passel of mo'ners on foot." The old woman fetched a little resigned sigh. "Well," she said, "I certainly wish I was settin' turned round the other way. I'd like mightily to see that there fun'el."

Mama had taken little Jerry with her on a shopping expedition. She was about to buy a thousand-dollar fur coat, when Jerry tugged at her skirt and announced, "Mommy, I gotta go." "Wait," commanded mommy. "No, I gotta go now," he insisted.

Anxious to consummate the sale, the proprietress of the shop volunteered, "I'll take him, madam."

When they returned, the mother commanded, "Now thank the nice lady for being so nice to you."

"I don't need to thank her," said little Jerry. "She had to go, too."

"I wish a book was like a play," said Ferenc Molnar when he turned the manuscript of a new novel over to his publishers on a hot summer day. "If a play is faltering, all you have to do is slap two words on the marquee and everything is lovely." "Tell me the two words," suggested his publisher, "and we'll put them on the book jacket." "That would not be practical," said Molnar, mopping his brow. "The two words are 'air conditioned.'"

Two brothers became owners of a country house through a joint inheritance. One, a go-getter and social climber, spent more than he could afford to fill his half of the house with the last word in decorations and mechanical devices. The other brother left his half exactly as he had found it, and simply enjoyed himself on it. "This is unfair," grumbled the first one. "You owe it to me to do something with your part of the house, as I have done with mine." "Very well," said his brother, thoroughly fed up. "I *will* do something with my half. I'll set it on fire." He did.

Mme. Schumann-Heink was the soloist at a Chicago concert one afternoon, and had to make her entrance via a narrow aisle between the violins and 'cellos. She found the going very difficult, and one musician, endeavoring to be helpful, suggested, "Why don't you try going sideways?" The portly diva gave him a despairing look and snorted, "Mein Gott! Don't you see I *haff* no sideways?"

There was a bit of high drama last year in that most unexpected of places, the annual meeting of a big Wall Street bank. The pompous chairman introduced a speaker with whom he was obviously unfamiliar as "one of the distinguished vice-presidents of our institution." The gentleman in question flushed with anger and began his address by assuring the assemblage, "I resent being called a vice-president of the institution. I am the fourth assistant cashier."

Three young sprouts from a prominent publishing house lunched at a crowded Automat one Monday. The only table with three seats available was already pre-empted by a formidable old lady, whose presence put a decided damper on the exchange of tall tales of week-end conquests they all had been looking forward to. One of the crafty subeditors had an idea.

"I promised my girl I'd take a bath Saturday night," he said with a wink to his companion. "It'll be exactly a year since I took one last."

"Well, well," said the second. "If that's the case, I think I'll change my socks. I threw them up to the ceiling this morning, and the left one stuck there for five minutes."

"Youse boids sound like Y.W.C.A. convoits," sneered the third (a graduate *cum laude* of Harvard). "I ain't been in a tub for tree years. I *love* doit."

The three brilliant plotters looked hopefully at the old lady, but she placidly continued munching her pie. Then she poured cream into her coffee, and spoke for the first time. "Would one of you stinkers," she said, "kindly pass me the sugar?"

For her act in the Persian Room at the Plaza, the ebullient Hildegarde always summons a gentleman from a ringside table to the microphone for a bit of spontaneous badinage. One evening she selected a dapper little fellow, and said, "I'll bet you're a perfume salesman." "Not a chance," he told her. "Matter of fact, I'm a retired pugilist." "Amazing," was Hildegarde's comment. "How could you ever hit anybody with those delicate little hands?" "I never did, lady," he admitted. "That's why I'm retired."

Little Linda checked with her mother. "You told me, Mommy, that angels have wings and can fly, didn't you?" "Yes, I did," said the mother. "Well," said Linda, "last night I heard Daddy calling my nurse an angel. When is she going to fly?" The mother answered promptly. "Tomorrow morning, darling."

My Uncle Herbert from Vermont took his New York Guide Book back to the Johnny Appleseed Bookshop for credit the day he returned from his first visit to the big city. "Things was bustin' loose so fast right thar in the depot," he explained, "that I never did get up to the village!"

"Now that you ask, Judge," said the defendant with downcast eyes, "I guess I never did earn an honest dollar. But there was that two bits you gave me to vote for you last——." "Case dismissed," roared the Judge.

A wonderful incident occurred at the Washington airport in the very last days of World War II. An Iranian air mission flew in for a series of informal discussions about the postwar aviation setup. The Iranian minister sent a high dignitary to represent his countrymen, of course, and the Air Transport Command was represented by Major General George. The Iranian mistook the latter for General Marshall and addressed him so three or four times. Finally, General George decided to set him right. "The name, sir," he said somewhat distantly, "is George." The Iranian smiled happily, bowed from the waist, and responded, "Please call me Mohammed."

Mrs. Wilson left her gloves, as usual, in the restaurant. She discovered her loss at the door and turned back. They weren't on the table, so she got down on all fours and began to search underneath. A waiter tapped her on the shoulder. "If it's your husband you're looking for, madam," he said respectfully, "I think you'll find him in the washroom."

In Pasadena, two ladies with Harvard accents were overheard in Vroman's Bookstore. "Heavens, this heat is enervating," complained one. "Don't forget," reproved the other, "that you're 3000 miles from the ocean." . . .

In Houston, a sweet young thing ordered a copy of *What Every Girl Should Know*, phoned the next morning to substitute *The Care and Feeding of Infants*. . . .

In London, Noel Coward gave a prominent novelist the brusheroo. "Last year you raved about him," a companion reminded him. "Ah, yes," said Coward. "First the fever, then the rash."

I never fail to shudder at the story of the two drunks who appropriated a Cadillac coupé and went tearing up Broadway at the height of the theatre crush at sixty miles an hour. "Thish ish terrible," cried the passenger. "I can't stand it." "Okay, then," counseled the driver. "Jush close your eyes like I'm doing."

Another version of the same yarn has the passenger exclaiming, "For Pete's sake, look where you're driving," with the loon at the wheel answering, "Am I driving? I thought you were."

Two other gents, rather obviously under the influence, were hauled into court at Coney Island one Sunday. "All I was doing, Your Honor," protested the first, "was picking up pebbles." "And me, I was just helping," chimed in the other. "Officer," said the judge, "is what these men say true? If so, I don't see why they merited arrest." "Your Honor," said the policeman grimly, "you shoulda gotta look at Pebbles!"

The guests in a Cairo hotel were awakened one night by wild screaming in the corridor. They discovered a beautiful damsel in extreme negligee fleeing madly from a gentleman who was, to put it bluntly, nude. The next day it developed that the impetuous Romeo was an English Major and he promptly was court-martialled. His lawyer won him an acquittal, however, by virtue of the following paragraph in the Army Manual: "It is not compulsory for an officer to wear a uniform at all times, as long as he is suitably garbed for the sport in which he is engaged."

One of the authors of *Girl Crazy* encountered George Gershwin's father at intermission time of the première. (George, of course, had composed the score.) "Think it's going well?" asked the author. "My boy," Papa Gershwin assured him, "it's a smack."

No patriot would try to underestimate the contributions our Puritan forefathers made to early American history, but the fact must be faced that a gloomier lot of killjoys never drew breath. They came here to worship in their own way—and to make everybody else do the same! One historian's caustic summation was "A Puritan is a man who is sincerely repentant for other people's sins." The Pilgrims faced similar hardships, but managed to have some fun and merrymaking on the side. The Puritans called them flibbedy-gibbets.

Macaulay notes that when the Puritans were in the saddle in England, they suppressed the popular sport of bearbaiting. "They did not do it," he explains, "because it gave pain to the bear, but because it gave pleasure to the spectators." Some three hundred years later, Henry Adams wrote, "Thank God, I never was cheerful. I come from Puritan stock. My ancestors passed their mornings reflecting on the goodness of God and the damnation of infants."

We have the Puritan influences to thank for our most ridiculous blue laws, self-appointed "suppression of vice" societies, and other busybodies whose lives are devoted to keeping other people from enjoying themselves. The Puritan philosophy is summed up in the reaction of the Salem maid in witch-hunting days who, kissed by her lover for the first time, burst into wild tears and lamented "This must be a terrible, terrible sin, John. It makes me feel so good!"

Marlin Hurt says that the first time he met his wife, he was standing in a drugstore. "What a moment! I heard a buzzing in my ears, bells sounded, and lights flashed. You know what that means!" "I sure do," answered his straight-man. "You must have been leaning against a pinball machine!"

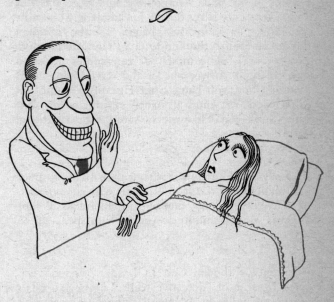

On her deathbed, the beautiful Hollywood star burst into tears, and whispered weakly to her industrialist husband, "Oh, Hector, you've been so good to me, and I've been such a bad girl! I've been unfaithful to you a hundred times!" "Don't excite yourself," said the husband calmly. "Who do you think put the cyanide in your coffee?"

Everybody knows what a WAC is (or was), but only the favored few know the meaning of a WOC. It's something you thwow at a wabbit.

On one of the sillier radio quiz programs, where they give a man twenty silver dollars for knowing who wrote Gray's *Elegy*, a sailor was baffled by the question "How do you finish the line reading 'Humpty Dumpty sat on a ——'?" The master of ceremonies, eager to worm the right answer out of the serviceman, urged "Come on, boy, you know what Humpty Dumpty sat on, don't you?" "I know all right," said the sailor, "but I don't think you'd like me to say it over a national hookup."

They say Mr. Fleischman personally is trying to track down the phone operator in his plant who answers calls with a cheery "Good morning! Fleischman Baking Company! Which crumb do you wish to speak to?"

A nominee of the late Carter Glass for Annapolis was rejected because of "defective teeth." Outraged, Glass sought out Charles F. Adams, Republican Secretary of the Navy, and expostulated, "You don't expect him to bite the enemy, do you?" "If you Democrats keep slashing our Navy appropriations," answered Adams, "he may have to."

A doctor at a free dispensary examined a vaudeville actor and then handed him three pills. "Take one after every meal," he prescribed, "and let me know if there is any improvement." A month later the doctor met the actor on the street and said angrily, "Why haven't you come in to report to me?" The actor said, "You told me to take a pill after every meal, didn't you? You gave me three pills, didn't you? Well, I've still got two pills left."

Benjamin Franklin once was showing some visitors the sights of Philadelphia, when a group of Quakers sauntered by. "I've never seen costumes like that," remarked one visitor. "Who are those people?" "Quakers," said Franklin. "What do they believe?" asked the visitor. Franklin answered promptly, "They believe in six per cent compound interest."

Miraqulo the Masked Marvel, known to his friends as Mike Shlivowitz, parked his 394-pound carcass wearily on the doctor's couch and moaned, "Oh, Doc, what happened to me when I wrestled the Mighty Nabisco shouldn't happen to an agent." "What went wrong?" said the doctor. "We were all mixed up in the middle of the ring," explained Miraqulo, "and I wasn't getting none the better of it. Suddenly a great big fanny stares me in the face and I says to myself, 'Mike, here's your chance.' So I takes a good healthy bite out of it." "Wasn't that against the rules?" said the doctor. "It was not only against the rules," moaned Miraqulo, "but it was my fanny!"

The chemist looked up from the analysis of the home-made hooch a cautious Scotchman had submitted, and said "I'm sorry, but this stuff is awful. Two drinks, and I guarantee you would be blind for life.

Better let me destroy it." "No need to do that," said the Scotchman. "My old friend McGregor, who's been blind all his life, lives just round the corner. Might as well gi'e it to him for a birthday present."

A simple soul who had read a lot of pigeon stories in previous compilations of jokes, wandered into Central Park one afternoon and managed to grab hold of one of the pigeons who was strutting on the Mall. He spent ten fruitless minutes trying to get the pigeon to talk to him and then, with an ejaculation of disgust, let it escape. "Just my luck," he muttered, "to get hold of one of the deaf and dumb ones."

The quick-tempered Clarence Day, author of *Life with Father*, was once taken ill at a summer resort. His wife, very much against his will, summoned the local doctor. That night she demanded "Clarence, did you follow that physician's prescription?" "If I had," snorted Day, "they'd probably be treating me for a broken neck, because I threw it down three flights of stairs."

Ella Wheeler Wilcox once sold a magazine a poem that began, "My soul is a lighthouse keeper." The day the magazine was published she charged into the editor's office with fire in her eyes. The printer, it seemed, had set up the line to read "My soul is a light house-keeper."

Two German students got into a fight, over the philosophy of Spinoza of all things, and according to the Heidelberg code, had to fight a duel. Both of them were physical cowards, however, and cannily stipulated that the duel be waged with pistols—and in the dark. Fritz won the toss, and shot first. He groped about the blacked-out room and finally managed to discharge his weapon up the chimney place. He scored a bullseye— catching his adversary squarely in the seat of his pants!

There was a sad incident one day in the heart of the Ozark Mountains. A farmer's mule kicked his mother-in-law to death. A tremendous crowd turned out for the funeral, but it was made up almost entirely of men. The minister commented, "This old lady must have been mighty popular because so many people will leave their work to come to her funeral."

"They're not here for the funeral," said the surprised farmer. "They're here to buy the mule."

Bert Leston Taylor, whose "Always in Good Humor" column in the Chicago *Tribune* was the forerunner of a horde of imitators operating today, once taxed a reporter friend on the *News* with the charge that the *Tribune* personnel was much more honest than the crew on the *News*. "You'll have to prove that statement," said the *News* man angrily. "Gladly," said Taylor. "I left a ham sandwich on my desk at the *Tribune* for two hours the other day. Did anybody touch it? No! On the other hand, while I was waiting here in your office for you, I noticed half a bottle of Scotch on your desk. I drank it. I tell you, my boy, you *News* fellows will have to mend your ways."

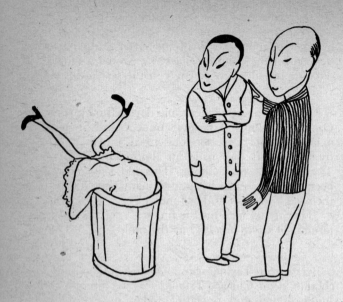

Higginbottom's divorce case established the fact pretty clearly that he had frequently mistaken his bride for a punching bag, and had once dumped her head-first into a garbage can. (Yes, it was at that precise moment that the traditional Chinese student went by and remarked to a colleague, "Amellican extlavagance! She good for ten years yet.")

Judge Wallace said sternly, "Higginbottom, you're a disgrace to your sex. I've decided to give your wife sixty dollars a week."

"That's mighty white of you, Judge," allowed Higginbottom. "I'll try to slip her a buck or two once in a while myself."

Two young rips from Oxford came up to London for a riotous week end. After some hours of dissipation in a West End cinema, they picked up two ladies of the evening on Piccadilly, and repaired to a neighboring pub, where, for reasons of their own, the two couples separated. A short while later, however, Bertie was back, tapping on his friend's shoulder. "I say, old man," he began, with a slightly embarrassed air. "Would you mind terribly swapping girls with me? What with this bloody fog and all, I seem to have got hold of my bloody aunt!"

A manufacturer inspected his wife's new bathing suit, and remarked caustically, "Shirley, it is just big enough to prevent your being tanned where you ought to be."

A visitor from Binghamton looked at the theatre tickets his broker had saved for him, and philosophized, "Z row, eh? At least, it ought to be the coolest part of the house."

Everybody was very nice to the American gentleman before the fox hunt began, but back at the manor house that evening they cut him dead. Baffled, the American sought an explanation from his host. That worthy, with an expression of acute distaste on his face, unbent sufficiently to say, "In this part of Sussex, my good man, when we are hunting, and corner the fox, the expression used is 'Tally-ho!'—not 'There goes the little son of a b—— now.'"

Sign discovered by Ben Allen in a Second Avenue delicatessen: "If you can't smell it, we ain't got it."

"My most humiliatin' experience," Jimmy Durante told his radio audience, "come the day a brat at the circus starts shovin' peanuts up my schnozzola. I ups to him and says, 'Desist, you is annoying me.' The brat pokes the woman he's wid and says, 'Whaddya know! Dis elephant kin talk!'"

Waxing philosophical, Jimmy pointed out that his famous oversized nose was far from a liability. "I am probably the only man in the country," he declared, "who can keep a cigar lit while he takes a shower."

A bumpkin was brought to Dr. Samuel Johnson's table in a tavern one night, and having heard of Johnson's savage wit in advance, played safe by roaring with laughter at everything the Doctor said. One shattering guffaw finally exhausted Johnson's patience. "I must be in terrible form tonight," he grumbled. "This imbecile seems to comprehend everything I say."

An old Negro was sentenced to five years in the penitentiary. The judge asked him if he had anything to say. The old man inquired, "Ain't you bein' a bit liberal with my time?"

Alan Reed (who created the role of Falstaff on the Fred Allen program) explained that he had changed his name from Bergman. "Where could I get with a name like Bergman?" he asked. "Who knows?" was the reply. "Ingrid Reed seems to be doing all right."

A story that appears in an old English miscellany published in 1841 (sent to me by Fred Schang of the Metropolitan Concert Bureau), and that probably dates back even further than that, is still standing vaudeville monologists in good stead.

The latest version begins with a wealthy planter returning from a trip to New York, and greeting the faithful retainer at the station with a "Well, you old rascal, anything happen at the estate while I was gone?" "Nuthin wuth mentionin', boss," answers the retainer cheerily, " 'Cept, of course de two hands what died fum eatin' all dat burnt hoss flesh."

"Where on earth did they get hold of burnt horse flesh?"

"Dat was when de stables caught fire, boss."

"The stables?"

"Yassuh! Sparks fum de big house, dey figger."

"The big house! Sparks! How did the fire start?"

"Fum de candles round de coffin, suh. Place burned to de groun' afore we could do a thing."

"Good heavens, man! Whose coffin?"

"Your ma, boss. I s'pect she died fum de shock."

"What shock?"

"Yo' wife, boss. She done ran away wid de butler."

Carole Landis is the Hollywood glamour girl who put fresh meaning into the word "curvaceous." Sid Skolsky, the connoisseur, thinks so too. On the Twentieth Century-Fox lot one day he assured her, "Honey, you look like a million dollars and you sure have got the money invested in the right places."

"What an expense I had in Miami Beach this winter," moaned a returned sun worshipper. "A fifty-dollar tip for two uppers going down. Then my wife insists on a hotel that charges thirty-five dollars a day with one glass of orange juice thrown in. Then the sun is too hot for her on the beach the first morning and I find her unconscious." "What did you do for her?" inquired his partner. The man admitted, "I put her on a train back to New York."

Giuseppe practically had his first papers in his pocket when the magistrate stumped him with a simple question about the American flag. "Come, come," said the magistrate sympathetically. "What is it you always see flying over this courthouse?" "Pigeons," said Giuseppe triumphantly.

A drunk was weaving through the Bronx Zoo one day when a lion broke out of his cage. People scattered wildly in every direction, but the drunk calmly walked up to the lion, grabbed him by the mane, and marched him back to his quarters.

The next day the mayor called him and said, "We're having a medal struck off for you. Collaring a lion empty-handed is about the greatest act of bravery I know." The hero, now sober, clapped a hand to his head. "Great Jehosophat," he cried. "Don't tell me that lion was real"—and fainted.

"Bopping your bride over the head with a lead pipe just isn't done any longer in Colorado," said the judge. "Ten years in the cooler to learn better manners." "But your honor," the defendant protested. "It wasn't no lead pipe. It was a shovel." "A shovel, eh?" said the judge. "In that case we'll make the sentence *twenty* years. Spades are double."

"De lodge meetin' had to be postponed las' night," an old darky told his boss. "De Supreme Exalted Invincible Unlimited Sixty-ninth Degree Potentate's wife jes' wouldn' let him come!"

Mrs. Kelly, having presented the world and her husband with triplets, was resting comfortably at the hospital when her friend, Mrs. O'Reilly, came to call.

"Triplets!" exclaimed Mrs. O'Reilly. "Faith and it's a wonderful thing, havin' one's family all at once-like instead of one at a time like common folks."

"Aye, that it is, that it is, Mrs. O'Reilly," beamed the proud mother. "You know the doctors says it happens only once in two hundred thousand times."

Mrs. O'Reilly, visibly impressed, shook her head and said, "Saints above and is that a fact now? If I'm not bein' overcurious, Mrs. Kelly, WHIN did you be after findin' time to do the housework?"

On the late Major Bowes' amateur hour (remember?) a little Chinese girl was once introduced who informed the Major that her father was a painter. "House painter?" he asked. "Just fine," the little Chinese girl replied.

Mrs. Taylor thought the doctor was overcharging for seeing her son through a siege of the measles. "Don't forget," the doctor reminded her, "that I visited your son eleven times." "But don't you forget," she countered, "that he infected the whole school."

After ten years in the booby hatch, a patient was declared sane by the authorities, and ready to face the rigors of the postwar world. As a last test he was allowed to shave with a straight razor, a privilege never before allowed him. The patient began shaving in front of a mirror that hung from the ceiling on a string. As he shaved he began to describe to the guard what things he expected to do as soon as he was free. He became more and more animated as he talked. Finally, in turning to face the guard, he made a wide sweeping gesture with the razor and cut the mirror down. When he saw what he had done, he burst into violent tears.

"It's not that bad," soothed the guard. "What are you crying about?"

"I am the unluckiest man in the world," sobbed the patient. "After ten years in this place they tell me I am cured and that I can go home, and now look what I did to myself. I cut my head off."

"The worst insult I ever got in radio," admits Bob Hope, "came from my pal Crosby. He phoned after my broadcast and said, 'Either you get off the air, or I stop breathing!'"

The Southern Boulevard Pinochle and Parchesi Club was raided by the police for the fourth time, and Mrs. Pincus, vice-president, knocked over two cops in her rush for the patrol wagon. "De lest two times," she explained, "I hed to stend all de way to de station house."

A Camp Dix correspondent swears this actually happened during the let-down period that followed V-J Day. The commanding officer of the post entered the barber shop in the middle of the afternoon and found one of his assistants getting a haircut. He remarked caustically, "I see you're getting your hair cut on government time, eh?" "Yes, sir; it grew on government time," pointed out the assistant. "Not all of it," pursued the C. O. "Right, sir," agreed the unperturbed assistant. "I'm not getting all of it cut off."

Bob Burns reports the case of the unhappy mountaineer whose son was marched off to school by the truant officer. "Larnin'!" mocked the mountaineer. "Fiddlesticks! Why, they're teachin' my poor boy to spell 'taters with a P!"

To illustrate the point that a ham actor simply cannot help exaggerating, Abel Green, wily editor of *Variety*, cites the story of the old star who found himself involved in one of the most disastrous failures of the season. The second night the boxoffice took in exactly eight dollars. The star saw there was no use trying to conceal the facts from his pals at the Lambs Club, so he decided to put on a bold front. "I think the take tonight must have been the lowest gross in Broadway history," he confided. "Just think! Only *sixteen* bucks!"

Abel calls the reporters on his staff "My Muggs." One of the youngest, he admits, has Tarzan eyes: "They swing from limb to limb." To get his mind off the girls, Abel took him on a sunny afternoon to the Central Park Zoo. The mugglet pointed at one animal and said, "I can see now why they call that a giraffe. Look at the long neck it has."

"Yes, sir," asserted Mr. Ekhamer vehemently—perhaps a shade *too* vehemently, "my wife is just as beautiful today as she was when I married her twenty years ago." Then he added, "Of course, it takes her longer."

Sandy McTavish (inspiration for Ogden Nash's immortal couplet, "No McTavish was ever lavish") returned from Palm Beach with a magnificent tan, as expected, and an alligator on a leash, altogether unexpected. McTavish explained affably, "I'm nae gaun to lose sight of him. He gobbled my golf ball at the river-r-r hole!"

Apartments were getting harder and harder to find in town, so Mrs. Kramer was understandably elated when she reported to her husband the discovery of an empty flat. When Mr. Kramer examined it he objected, "But dearie, this house is right next to the main line of the Pennsylvania Railroad. It will take us six months to get used to the roar and rumble." Mrs. Kramer reflected for a moment, and then said brightly, "That won't be so bad, darling. We can sleep the first six months at mama's house."

News item from the Phoenix *Flame:* "Miss Fay King was overcome by gas while taking a bath. She owes her life to the watchfulness of the janitor of her apartment building."

There were two thousand well-fed and well-lubricated guests in the banquet hall, making a formidable racket, and the worried chairman said to Cass Daley, "I hope you can sing loud enough to make this gang hear you." "Sing loud enough," laughed Miss Daley. "Son, I'm the only songbird who ever got an answer from Chloe."

Mrs. Bigelow was seeing her infant grandson for the first time. "You scrumptious, angelic thing," she cooed. "Won't it speak to its little gramikins?" The infant scowled and muttered, "How the hell do you expect me to talk when I'm only two months old?"

Uncle Rastus carefully spelled out the inscription on a tombstone: "Not dead but sleeping." He chuckled and remarked to his wife, "Dat colored boy ain't foolin' nobody but hisself."

A timid lady boarded a Philadelphia local at Trenton and asked the conductor, "Does this train stop at Broad Street Terminal?" "If it doesn't, lady," he assured her, "you're going to see one hell of a crash!"

"Oh dear," sighed the movie starlet at Romanoff's. "If only I weren't on a diet! Is banana shortcake really fattening?" The suave Prince Michael smiled and assured her, "Only if you eat it."

There are all kinds of golf caddies in the world, says Bobby Jones, but the venerable and dignified veterans at the famous St. Andrews course in Scotland are in a class by themselves. One of these caddies, 75 if he was a day, found himself assigned to an irascible duffer who blamed everybody but himself for his atrocious playing. After five tortuous holes, he stepped up to the tee and sliced his ball at a perfect right angle to the fairway into a dense thicket. "Better play another ball, sir," suggested the caddie. "That one's hopelessly lost." The duffer said angrily, "You're positively the worst caddie in the world." The old caddie said quietly, "Oh no, sir, that would be too great a coincidence."

If you can believe the statisticians of *Judge* magazine, what the scarf said to the hat was "You go ahead—I wanna neck." When the elephant sat down in the little stream, the latter murmured, "Well, I'm damned." One eye pointed out to the other eye, "Just between us, there's something that smells." The executioner confided as he pulled the switch, "This'll kill you." The key asked the keyhole, "What do you hear from the knob?" And one stocking said to its mate, "So long. I gotta run." High time too, if you ask me!

The opposition candidate concluded an intemperate and inept tirade with a bang of his fist on the table and a cry of "Are you going to take all this lying down?" "Not on your life," came a voice from the rear. "We've got shorthand reporters here for that."

A friend of George Heister, out in Pine Bluff, Arkansas, went to New York to hear what the insiders on the cotton exchange thought of the prospects. "Wire me the straight dope," asked Heister. In due course he received this telegram from his friend: "Some think it's going up. Some think it's going down. I agree. Whatever you do it will be wrong. Act at once."

Heedless of an impatient queue behind him, a Scotchman at a Grand Central ticket window counted his change very carefully three times.

The ticketseller watched him sourly. "Well," he said, "are you finally satisfied it's right?"

"Aye, mon," said the Scot angrily, "but only *just* right."

Lord Higglebotham was driving through the Adirondacks, and suddenly noticed a sign at the top of a steep grade that read, "Drive slowly. This means you!" "Wonderful country," mused the Lord. "How on earth did they know I was over here?"

Bernard Geis, Esquire's gift to Grosset and Dunlap, cultivates an advertising magnate principally to hear of one of his clients, a "dese and dem" character with a beautiful wife, a marble mansion slightly larger than the Pentagon Building, and a couple of million dollars in the bank.

One day the advertising man noticed that there were solid gold plates on the dinner table, and couldn't control a slight gasp of surprise. "What did you think?" asked the host, thoroughly annoyed. "Should we live like *pigs*?" In the drawing room later, the ad man admired a beautiful painting. "I see you have a Monet," he said: "You know," replied the art collector, "you're the *second person* who said that!"

There was one time when the millionaire lost his sang froid. He came home unexpectedly and found his pin-up bride making violent love to a total stranger on the divan. For days he was wild with distraction. He loved his wife far too much to contemplate divorce. Suddenly he found the perfect solution. He threw out the divan.

The Cedars of Lebanon Hospital in Hollywood notifies the entire staff when an interesting post-mortem is about to be performed. The event is subtly advertised over the loud-speaker system by a dulcet-voiced nurse who murmurs "Calling Dr. Post! Calling Dr. Mortimer Post!"

The last word on a metropolitan football team that went through an entire season without scoring a point was voiced by a prominent alumnus: "I wouldn't let my mother-in-law carry the ball behind that line."

The village blacksmith was mighty as all get-out, possibly because he stood under the very spreading chestnut tree that most of these jokes came from. Nevertheless he had trouble finding an apprentice who would put up with the hard labor and the low pay. He finally got hold of one recruit, husky enough, but with a suspi-

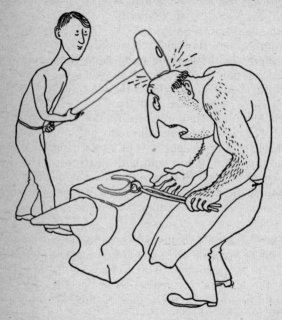

ciously blank look in his eyes. The blacksmith carefully explained, "Now I'll bring the shoe from the fire and lay it on this anvil. When I nod my head you smash it with this hammer."

The apprentice did exactly what he was told. Now *he's* the village blacksmith.

The head man of one of the biggest film studios on the Coast is tendered a banquet every year at which everybody waxes highly emotional, and superlatives are tossed about with reckless abandon. Guests prepare their "spontaneous remarks" weeks in advance.

This year, due to an unfortunate oversight, a world-famous novelist, temporarily employed to supervise the translation of his latest tear-jerker to scenario form, was not called upon to say his few words. The toastmaster, bemoaning his carelessness at a Beverly Hills bar later on, admitted, "What makes the episode doubly unfortunate is that he spent the entire afternoon in the make-up department having a lump put in his throat."

"Why is it," pondered Mr. Kendall, "that a woman is utterly incapable of writing a letter without a postscript tacked on to it?"

"As usual," answered his wife loftily, "you are talking nonsense. I'll write you a letter without a postscript just to cut you down to size."

The next morning her note arrived. Just below her signature he discovered, "P. S. Now are you convinced?"

An intrepid hunter was asked by one of the boys round the cracker barrel to recount his most hair-raising experience.

"It was deep in the woods back yonder," he began with no particular reluctance. "I was plodding along minding my own business when suddenly a huge grizzly bear sneaked up behind me. He pinned my arms to my sides and started to squeeze the breath out of me. My gun fell out of my hands. First thing you know the bear had stooped down, picked up the gun, and was pressing it into my back."

"What did you do?" chorused the audience on cue.

"What could I do?" sighed the hunter. "I married his daughter."

THE END

STOP!
DON'T READ
TOO MANY
JOKES AT ONE TIME.
THEY'RE FUNNIER IN SMALL DOSES

BANTAM BOOKS

The famous mysteries, novels and books of humor, cartoons and non-fiction listed here are all available through the dealer from whom this Bantam Book was purchased.

1. LIFE ON THE MISSISSIPPI, Mark Twain, *non-fiction*
2. THE GIFT HORSE, Frank Gruber, *mystery*
3. "NEVADA," Zane Grey, *Western*
4. EVIDENCE OF THINGS SEEN, Elizabeth Daly, *mystery*
5. SCARAMOUCHE, Rafael Sabatini, *novel*
6. A MURDER BY MARRIAGE, Robert George Dean, *mystery*
7. THE GRAPES OF WRATH, John Steinbeck, *novel*
8. THE GREAT GATSBY, F. Scott Fitzgerald, *novel*
9. ROGUE MALE, Geoffrey Household, *adventure*
10. SOUTH MOON UNDER, Marjorie Kinnan Rawlings, *novel*
11. MR. AND MRS. CUGAT, Isabel Scott Rorick, *humor*
12. THEN THERE WERE THREE, Geoffrey Homes, *mystery*
13. THE LAST TIME I SAW PARIS, Elliot Paul, *non-fiction*
14. WIND, SAND AND STARS, Antoine de Saint-Exupéry, *non-fiction*
15. MEET ME IN ST. LOUIS, Sally Benson, *humor*
16. THE TOWN CRIED MURDER, Leslie Ford, *mystery*
17. SEVENTEEN, Booth Tarkington, *humor*
18. WHAT MAKES SAMMY RUN? Budd Schulberg, *novel*
19. ONE MORE SPRING, Robert Nathan, *romance*
20. OIL FOR THE LAMPS OF CHINA, Alice Tisdale Hobart, *novel*
21. MEN, WOMEN AND DOGS, James Thurber, *cartoons*
22. BABBITT, Sinclair Lewis, *novel*
23. THE FOG COMES, Mary Collins, *mystery*
24. VALIANT IS THE WORD FOR CARRIE, Barry Benefield, *romance*
25. BUGLES IN THE AFTERNOON, Ernest Haycox, *Western*
26. NET OF COBWEBS, Elisabeth Sanxay Holding, *mystery*
27. ONLY YESTERDAY, Frederick Lewis Allen, *non-fiction*
28. NIGHT IN BOMBAY, Louis Bromfield, *novel*

ABSOL

ANYT

FO

LAU